"I've been waiting for this boo[...] [...]?
brings a fresh perspective to t[...] [...]
alive with hope of liberation fo[...] [...]s
us past the superficial into a deep engagement with a contextual
theology that is relevant and life-giving. We must rethink how to
address the racial and social injustices taking place in the world
today, and I am convinced that the way forward is womanist! So if
you want to become brave enough to move from being a concerned
bystander to an active participant—this book is for you! I highly
recommend it."

— **Brenda Salter McNeil**
author of *Becoming Brave:*
Finding the Courage to Pursue Racial Justice Now

"Dr. Parker understands the power of testimony to speak truth. This
book marks a path away from death-dealing forms of scholarly formation in evangelical biblical studies and toward thriving life in a
field and for a field. Parker's powerful text adds greatly to a growing
number of theologically rich antiracist and antisexist resources for
addressing our current struggles. Now we have yet another weapon
of righteousness."

— Willie James Jennings
author of *After Whiteness: An Education in Belonging*

"This book invites readers to embrace justice and Black Lives Matter by taking them on a journey of personal re-membering and critical reflection toward a womanist consciousness. Dr. Parker employs
the metaphorical language of God-breath (inspired scriptures) and
breathing (liberating interpretation that embraces all bodies and
blackness) unobstructed by the suffocating, breath-taking authoritarian claims of whiteness-centered biblical scholarship buttressed
by doctrinal claims of inerrancy and infallibility."

— **Mitzi J. Smith**
author of *Womanist Sass and Talk Back:*
(In)Justice, Intersectionality, and Biblical Interpretation

"What might the church be like if we were a people who walked with each other so well that we all 'made it home'? In this spirit (*ruach*)-filled book, Dr. Angela Parker calls with courage for us to release the white supremacist authoritarianism of inerrancy and infallibility. She invites with vision for us to journey into a living relationship with the Bible, one in which we need not—and, in fact, *must* not—leave our embodied experiences and identities behind. This book offers womanist air, as vital as it is 'God-breathed.'"

— Jennifer Harvey
author of *Dear White Christians:*
For Those Still Longing for Racial Reconciliation

If God Still Breathes, Why Can't I?

Black Lives Matter and Biblical Authority

Angela N. Parker

WILLIAM B. EERDMANS PUBLISHING COMPANY

GRAND RAPIDS, MICHIGAN

Wm. B. Eerdmans Publishing Co.
4035 Park East Court SE, Grand Rapids, Michigan 49546
www.eerdmans.com

27 26 25 24 23 22 21   1 2 3 4 5 6 7

ISBN 978-0-8028-7926-4

Library of Congress Cataloging-in-Publication Data

Names: Parker, Angela N., 1971– author.
Title: If God still breathes, why can't I? : Black Lives Matter and biblical
    authority / Angela N. Parker.
Description: Grand Rapids, Michigan : William B. Eerdmans Publishing
    Company, 2021. | Includes bibliographical references and index. |
    Summary: "A challenge to the doctrine of biblical inerrancy and its
    role in propagating White supremacist authoritarianism in the Chris-
    tian church"—Provided by publisher.
Identifiers: LCCN 2021007967 | ISBN 9780802879264 (paperback)
Subjects: LCSH: Race relations—Biblical teaching. | White supremacy
    movements—Religious aspects—Christianity. | Authoritarianism—
    Religious aspects—Christianity. | Black lives matter movement—
    Religious aspects—Christianity. | Racism—Religious aspects—
    Christianity. | Womanist theology. | Bible. New Testament—Criticism,
    interpretation, etc. | Bible—Evidences, authority, etc. | United States—
    Race relations.
Classification: LCC BS680.R2 P37 2021 | DDC 261.8/3—dc23
LC record available at https://lccn.loc.gov/2021007967

This book is dedicated to important maternal teachers:
my biological mother and first spiritual teacher, Argie L. Welch;
my doctoral mother, Seung Ai Yang;
and my Biblical Hebrew mother, Ellen F. Davis.
Thank you!

Contents

Foreword by Lisa Sharon Harper   ix

Preface   xiii

Acknowledgments   xv

Introduction:
What Is Your Relationship to the Bible?   1

1.   Stifled Breathing: Trained to Be a White Male
Biblical Scholar   13

2.   White Supremacist Authoritarianism
Is Not God's Breath   26

3.   Stop Gaslighting Me   44

4.   Moving from Stifled Breath to Full-Throated Faith   63

Conclusion:
Breathing Womanist Air   91

Appendix   101

Bibliography   103

Index   111

Foreword

I sat in the living room of my small 3.5-room apartment in Washington, DC. The documentary crew buzzed behind camera lights that washed the room in white light. They were there to conduct an interview for a documentary celebrating the five-hundred-year anniversary of the Protestant Reformation—that moment on October 31, 1517, when Martin Luther nailed his Ninety-five Theses to the door of All Saint's Church in Wittenberg, Germany. One does not have to be a scholar of Luther to understand the impact of that moment. Having endured the centuries-long conflict over papal authority between the Eastern and Western churches, Luther's Theses formed an earth-shattering crack inside Western Christianity. Five hundred years later, democratized Western Christianity is strewn with thousands of cracks, each forming a new denomination or "non-denomination."

As we closed the interview, the documentary director asked a simple question: What is the work of the church for the next five hundred years? My answer: If the first five hundred years after the Reformation was about the democratization of our faith, then the work of the next five hundred years will be its decolonization.

The Protestant Reformation was a particular event, in particular space, at a particular time, addressing particular issues that arose within a particular geographical, historical, and geopolitical context. The Reformation flowed from the lineage of Constantine—the state-based imperial European church. The Roman Church flowed from the Roman Empire, an arguably White supremacist empire. At the heart of the Roman Empire was the belief that its civilization was ordained to rule the world. Dr. Kelly Brown Douglas points out that Aristotle coined the term "western supremacy," which shaped Roman discourse and life and fueled the European imperial and colonial projects of the next two thousand years.

The pontifications of Reformation leaders were directly related to that lineage, rooted in the pattern and practice of domination, colonization, and imperial rule. The Ethiopian Church was also a state-based church, but it was not rooted in the patterns and practice of colonization and imperial rule. Thus, it developed differently as its scholars, theologians, and priests addressed different questions rising out of its particular context.

Context matters. The entirety of Scripture was written and originally read and heard within the context of the colonized or those under threat of colonization. Every single writer of the entire Bible was a colonized person, under its threat or recently released from slavery. Likewise, every single writer of Scripture was Brown. The color of their skin does not matter intrinsically. In the Hebrew Bible, all of the characters were Brown—both the colonists and the colonized. But the entire New Testament was written by Brown colonized Afro-Asian peoples in the context of the White and western supremacist Roman Empire. Color here is not about hues of the rainbow. It is about geopolitical context and power. It matters.

Likewise, the Protestant Reformation took place in a particular context. It took place within European struggles for power and dominance. It took place on the edge of the Age of Discovery, which quickly became the Age of Conquest and Slavery. Martin Luther nailed his Theses to the door in Wittenberg in 1517. The first slave ships sailed from Spain in the 1400s. Those ships did not traverse the Atlantic, but it did not take long. The first slave ship recorded in the Trans-Atlantic Slave Voyage database arrived at its destination in Vigo, Spain, in 1514, in the context of Catholic Spain—three years before Luther's Theses. Flip forward one century following Luther's monumental moment. Germany is entangled in global slavocracy, fueling its own economic well-being through industries that support the trade. Several German families financed Portuguese slave ships. One must face this simple truth: When a society's Christian faith—faith born from colonized and serially enslaved Brown people—does not cause that society to challenge and reject slavery outright, then there is a problem with the construction of that faith. To save our faith we must decolonize it.

In the tradition of James Cone, Katie Cannon, Renita Weems, Kelly Brown Douglas, Chanequa Walker-Barnes, and scores more, Angela Parker is among a rising generation of scholars carrying the project of decolonization squarely into the evangelical church. I spoke at the same conference that Parker references in her preface. I remember her talk and how gobsmacked I was to hear her articulate some of the same thoughts that had been taking root in me since the documentary interview in my living room. She articulated my thoughts through the lens of her own experience. Then she rooted them in research and sound biblical analysis. Though Parker does not identify as an evangelical, her scholarship has been located within that stream of the Christian church. And that stream has been overcome by White nationalist imperialism. Again, we declare: When a stream of the Christian faith—faith risen from the soil of colonized, serially enslaved Brown people— does not vehemently reject an attempted coup at the US Capitol where crosses, lynching ropes, and military gear find communion, then there is a problem with the construction of that faith. Parker calls this out and calls us to reimagine the man I have come to call Brown Jesus, and his mother, Brown Mary, and their ancestor, Brown David, and his hero, Brown Moses, and his ancestor, Brown Abraham, and his ancestor, Black Eve. What does it mean to follow Jesus when we strip Whiteness and westernness from his skin and the Brown colonized context from which he rose? What happens when those at the bottom read the words of those at the bottom? What suppressed, covered over, hidden, and obliterated meanings rise again? That is the project of the next five hundred years. Angela Parker's *If God Still Breathes* takes us one step further on the journey.

Lisa Sharon Harper

Preface

This book began when I was invited by Evangelicals 4 Justice to participate in a "Liberating Evangelicalism: Decentering Whiteness" conference that took place in September 2019. I spoke on the title "Decentering Whiteness in Biblical Scholarship." A listening and speaking body, Evangelicals 4 Justice describes itself as an eclectic network of evangelical thought leaders and activists dedicated to making a broad cultural impact through prophetic witness to the whole church. Its mission includes mobilizing evangelicals to engage a whole gospel in their personal lives and in the public square by doing justice, loving mercy, and walking humbly with God.

As an ordained Black Baptist minister and Womanist New Testament professor, I have never really thought of myself as "evangelical." However, after receiving my PhD, I quickly learned that folks in predominantly White institutions will label you if they offer you a job. My first appointment after completing my PhD was at the Seattle School of Theology and Psychology. The Seattle School understands itself as a "progressive evangelical" institution even though the nomenclature is undergoing disuse in the age of Trump.

I went to the "Liberating Evangelicalism" conference not knowing what to expect. I was shocked when my seemingly (in my mind) simple statement that "the doctrines of inerrancy and infallibility serve as tools of White supremacy" became the beginning of a yearlong process of outlining my thoughts. The book you hold in your hands is the beginning of this budding moment of research for me. Thank you for taking this journey with me.

Acknowledgments

B ooks begin when you least expect them to. The dominant influences in my life and career have been women who witnessed some spark within me and helped draw it out. However, one particular man saw some value in this present project. I want to thank Andrew Knapp, my acquisitions editor at Eerdmans, who recognized the validity of this project even before I recognized it. Second, I want to thank my dad, Robert C. Welch Sr., for listening to me complain about what it means to be a Womanist New Testament scholar tasked with teaching men who may not want to engage the New Testament in ways I consider necessary. Next, I want to thank Derek McNeil, who ended up being the best "first boss" I could ever imagine. Derek, you helped me see the value of my distinct and particular voice as I entered the "progressive evangelical" enclave of the Seattle School. Thank you. Finally, I have to acknowledge my spouse, Victor Parker. Victor, you are the partner that God knew I needed. You are not intimidated by my strong personality and opinions. You listen as I bounce ideas off you and off the walls of our home. You also make sure I walk away from writing and research when my eyes begin to blur and water. Thank you. Thank you for your love and grace even when I rail at my laptop and sometimes even at you!

Now I want to thank the women colleagues whose conversations with me have helped craft this work. Thank you, Alice Hunt, for being a powerful force in my life. Thank you, Chelle Stearns, for being an important conversation partner when I arrived at the Seattle School. We still need to write that book on unicorns! Thank you, too, to Stephanie Neil, O'Donnell Day, Caprice Hollins, Cheryl Goodwin, Kristen Houston, Rachel Chen, Kj Swanson, and Kate Rae Davis for our various conversations while Victor and I were in Seattle. I am also thankful for new colleagues in Chanequa Walker-Barnes, Nancy deClaissé-Walford, Karen Massey, Denise Massey, Michelle Garber, Nikki Hardeman, Diane Frazier, Beth Perry, and Marie Mathieu as I continue to acclimate myself to the Atlanta, Georgia, context. Thank you for continued collegial discourse as we all navigate what it means to be women in various types of leadership.

Finally, there are four New Testament scholars who continue to challenge me in our discussions, and I am extremely grateful for them. The first is Mitzi Smith. On many occasions, Mitzi has opened doors for writing, publication, and scholarly growth. Thank you. Also, thank you to Margaret Aymer for pointing me in directions that I did not even know I needed to go.

The last two are my ride-or-die partners in this academic endeavor. Sharon Jacob has become a great friend and conversation partner ever since our first meeting at a Wabash Center consultation. And Karri L. Whipple has been a friend, sister, and writing partner since our time at Union Theological Seminary. I look forward to writing that memoir later on. Thank you, friends, for helping me process some of the ideas in this book.

Introduction:
What Is Your Relationship to the Bible?

In every introductory New Testament class that I have taught in a seminary context, I begin the semester by asking students, "What is your relationship to the biblical text?" Oftentimes the answers vary. On one side of the spectrum is deep hostility toward and mistrust of the biblical text as a result of the ways the Bible has been used as a bludgeoning tool. This response comes mostly from the "nones"—those who identify as having no religious affiliation. Many of the nones who take my classes were raised evangelical and know the biblical text well but no longer want to engage it as sacred Scripture. You can imagine the joys of my job as their New Testament professor!

On the other side of the spectrum is an uncritical and wholehearted faith in the "infallible and inerrant truth of the Bible," in "the authoritative word of God." This response usually comes from conservative evangelical students who were raised in the Bible Belt and who want to engage in proper "orthodox" readings of the biblical text without engaging it in relation to the actual lived experience of Black bodies. Many such students have come to seminary after having attended a fundamentalist college where there were no Black women professors or after having already served as a pastor and thus are seeking a professor who rubberstamps what they think they already know about the biblical text.

These students know David as "a man after God's own heart," so why would I ask them to consider David as a rapist of Bathsheba or a negligent father to his raped daughter, Tamar? For these students, the story is not about Tamar but about David; they feel it's irrelevant to think about women in the Bible when *clearly* men are the important figures within the text. Their firm belief in so-called inerrancy and infallibility often means they read superficially without thinking about the hard questions of the text.

I recount these instances in order to begin to ground our time together in what I have identified as White supremacist authoritarianism within biblical interpretation. In my tenure as a professor, I have often witnessed African American students upholding an unshakeable faith in biblical infallibility that borders on White supremacy. Moreover, I've observed that students from the Bible Belt often do not think critically about their own liberation and are oftentimes complicit in promoting the same conservative attitudes that, I will argue, border on White supremacist authoritarianism. This book examines inerrancy and infallibility as tools of White supremacist authoritarianism that limit humanity's capacity to fully experience God's breath in the biblical text.

For me, particularly, I am a Womanist Christian wife to a strong Black man, Victor. I am the daughter of Robert and Argie. I am the mother of Ebony and Saron. I am the grandmother of Essence and Zayden. My family is identifiably and unapologetically Black. I am also a professor of the New Testament and yet . . . I can't breathe. I can't breathe because George Floyd could not breathe as a Minneapolis police officer literally kneed the life out of him on May 25, 2020. I can't breathe as I remember Eric Garner succumbing to a chokehold on a Staten Island street on July 17, 2014. I can't breathe because I want my grandchildren to be able to play in city parks without my having to worry about them being gunned down within two seconds like Tamir Rice on November 22, 2014. I can't breathe because I am constantly speaking the names of Trayvon Martin, Freddie Gray, Sandra Bland, Breonna Taylor, Walter Scott, Aiyana Stanley-Jones, Michael Brown, Laquan McDonald, Philando Castile, Stephon Clark, Ahmaud Arbery, Botham Jean, Atatiana Jefferson, Rekia Boyd, and so on and so on and so on. These are Black lives lost as a result of police authoritarianism that often goes unchecked as a result of qualified immunity for police officers. Since the founding of the United States of America, White Americans have demonstrated, generation after generation, that Black lives do not matter to them.

In the context of being a Womanist New Testament scholar, I often can't breathe as I wait for the White moderate student to question why I *always* center Black (and Brown) lives and bodies while reading and teaching the biblical text. In the context of being a Womanist New Testament scholar, I often can't breathe as I wait for a majority of my students to question their unstated assumptions about the inerrancy and infallibility of the biblical texts—doctrines that many hold dear. I have found in my early years of teaching that holding such doctrines as signs of personal piety often correlates to a student's unwillingness to engage Jesus Christ's crucifixion as a clarion call to social action against oppressive militarist systems.[1]

This book is my attempt to breathe in deeply the "God-breathed" biblical texts without doctrines of inerrancy and infallibility choking my breath. In essence, *If God Still Breathes, Why Can't I?* allows me to hold the idea of Scripture as authoritative while interrogating the doctrines of inerrancy and infallibility as tools of White supremacist thought that promote the erasure of communal memory. This book is written from the perspective of a

---

1. The cross of Jesus, I believe, demands Christians to engage social justice initiatives. For more on the interconnection between Jesus the crucified and Black humanity, see James H. Cone, *The Cross and the Lynching Tree* (Maryknoll, NY: Orbis, 2011). See also Cone's memoir, *Said I Wasn't Gonna Tell Nobody: The Making of a Black Theologian* (Maryknoll, NY: Orbis, 2018).

Womanist Christian who has questioned what her relationship to the biblical text is in the age of Black Lives Matter and the White supremacist authoritarianism that pervades American society since Donald Trump became president of the United States. In this work I do two things. First, I unapologetically interact with the Black Lives Matter movement as a way to synthesize reading of the biblical text with women and men who suffer consistently from police violence in the United States.[2] Second, I bring my own embodied identity as a Womanist scholar who teaches and preaches the gospel message of Jesus as the Christ while recognizing that sometimes the God-breathed authority of Scripture gets lost within the confines of White supremacist authoritarianism.

On June 1, 2020, the nation witnessed a prominent example of the Bible's being used as an instrument of White supremacist authoritarianism. On said day, President Donald Trump used military force to clear peaceful protesters in the District of Columbia—deploying police officers mounted atop horses and expending tear gas—so that he could pose for a photo in front of a burned church, holding a Bible as a prop. He did not make any remarks or read any text from the Bible. My own personal conversations with friends about the photo op yielded a spectrum of responses. Some touted President Trump as *the* president for their own particular brand of evangelical thinking and were ecstatic that he held a Bible. Others were shocked by the lack of critical engagement with the biblical text. As for me, I remember thinking that there is no evidence of "God breathing" in that moment.

2. There has been an increase in protests and the acknowledgment that Black Lives Matter is a legitimate protest movement by many since the killing of George Floyd on May 25, 2020, at the knee of a Minnesota police officer. Many across the world could not avert their gaze from the cell phone footage of the officer kneeling on Floyd's neck for nearly nine minutes while onlookers begged him to remove his knee. For an excellent exploration of the Black Lives Matter movement and its conversation with Black liberation, see Keeanga-Yamahtta Taylor, *From #BlackLivesMatter to Black Liberation* (Chicago: Haymarket Books, 2016).

This book is written by a Womanist New Testament scholar who expects to experience God's breath in the reading and hearing of the Bible. My relationship to the Bible is one of love, respect, and deep wrestling along with fierce defense when I see it used in public as a prop. I begin by acknowledging and emphasizing my relationship to the biblical text because this present book is a critical engagement with much of the history of biblical interpretation. I will question the adequacy of the doctrines of inerrancy and infallibility, showing the prominent way in which Christianity steeped in White supremacist authoritarianism responds to being called out on racism in its doctrines about the Bible. I also try to note how those doctrines have seeped into my own mind and body as a result of my training in biblical studies as a Black Christian woman. I will try to find ways in which we can excise these White supremacist ideas from our readings of the biblical text and de-center this thought in our faith communities today.

I hope this book finds a home within faith communities that share my love of deep wrestling, even if they, too, have at one time or other tossed the Bible in a corner out of frustration with the deeply ingrained White supremacist ideologies it has often been used to perpetuate. I also hope this book finds a home with readers who have a deep social justice stance in their faith walk and want to understand why. This book is written to begin to excise the White supremacist authoritarianism in all of us and within our biblical interpretations. Regardless of whether we identify as Black, African, African American, White, Asian, Latinx, or Indigenous, we have all had aspects of White supremacist authoritarianism take up residence in our minds and bodies. What will we do to remove it?

A Word on "White Supremacy" and "White Supremacist Authoritarianism"

Before we begin to exorcise the demons of White supremacist authoritarianism, I must begin with definitions. I use the language of "White supremacy" and "White supremacist authoritarianism" extensively to identify a system we all find ourselves in as we read biblical texts, especially within evangelical and mainline Protestant circles.

So what does "White supremacy" actually mean? According to Merriam-Webster, White supremacy is "a doctrine based on a belief that the White race is inherently superior to other races and that White people should have control over people of other races." I do believe "White supremacy" is an especially appropriate term to use when I engage evangelical and mainline Protestants along issues of race and biblical interpretation, because those who identify as White are the arbiters of power when it comes to biblical interpretation. For example, even if I am the faculty of record in a New Testament class, I can have my White (and often male) colleague guest-lecture in my class and state the exact same concepts I have previously lectured on, and students receive the White male colleague's lecture as truth. I know I am not the only woman professor or Black professor to experience such bias. Accordingly, defining "White supremacy" is important because it points to not just a belief but a foundation that places White people over others for the benefit of White identity.

In relationship to White supremacy, I employ the term "White supremacist authoritarianism" as distinct from the idea of "biblical authority." The concept of authority, as many feminists have already asserted, is problematic for women, as men often use the patriarchal ideas found in the Bible as a way to exert permanent and unquestionable authority over women.[3] For the purpose of this book, I use the term "authoritarianism" to emphasize that while not all authority is problematic, authoritarianism is, since it

---

3. An excellent work that delves into women and the issue of authority is Sarah Heaner Lancaster, *Women and the Authority of Scripture: A Narrative Approach* (Harrisburg, PA: Trinity Press International, 2002).

is a distorted or misguided use of authority. "White supremacist authoritarianism" in particular is the problematic and misguided use of authority based on an ideology steeped in White supremacy as defined above. I will make the argument that the doctrines of biblical inerrancy and biblical infallibility are inherently steeped in White supremacist authoritarianism.[4]

A Word on "Inerrancy" and "Infallibility"

The term "inerrant" simply means "free from error." Many evangelical and mainline Protestants employ the term as a way to describe what they feel is the "trustworthiness" of the biblical text as God's word. Congregations and individuals usually uphold that because God is trustworthy, the biblical text is trustworthy as well. In the history of the Protestant idea of Scripture, "inerrancy" means the Bible points humanity to the way of salvation. For some Protestants the biblical text is inerrant only in relationship to salvation. For others (that is, some strands of fundamental and conservative evangelicals) the Bible is completely accurate in whatever it teaches about all other subjects, such as science and history.

The related concept of "infallibility" is the characteristic of being incapable of failing to accomplish a predetermined purpose. The Protestant Reformers broke with the Catholic Church by stating that only the biblical text is infallible, whereas Catholic doctrine teaches that the teaching of the church under the

---

4. To be clear, I do not envision an idea of "White supremacist *authority*" that is "good"; White supremacist authority would be an evil as well. However, I do want to differentiate between "biblical authoritarianism" and "biblical authority." In future works I will address the biblical authoritarianism that Black women often experience at the hands of Black male pastors who are steeped in authoritarianism. However, that conversation is for another project.

authority of the pope, its earthly head, is infallible as well. Martin Luther and John Calvin are credited with correcting the abuses of the Catholic Church and bringing the authority of the biblical text to the forefront.

The problem with many evangelicals and mainline Protestants today stems from their belief that God inspired absolutely everything in the Bible according to these sixteenth-century ideas of inerrancy and infallibility. If that is the case, then every word on every page—every command, every idea, every scenario—is intended for and relevant to every single Christian who is reading the biblical text today. However, every single Christian must embody a particular White Protestant identity that, I argue, is found in most conservative White evangelical Christian circles. Since these White evangelicals bring so much of their own culture and personal lives to the Bible, there is no room for other engagement (such as Black Lives Matter) with the biblical text. In this way of thinking, there is room for only one particular life experience: a White life experience.

For such people, when others engage the biblical text from alternative perspectives or raise certain questions, it triggers a knee-jerk defensiveness. After lecturing on the Gospel of Matthew in my first year of teaching, for example, an older White conservative evangelical student began to *yell* at me after class for referring to the Scriptures as a "text." Did I have a problem referring to the Bible as "the word of God" or "sacred text"?! Said student also hurled, "How dare you question the character of Jesus in Matthew 15!" If you are unaware, Matthew 15:21–28 is the story where Jesus calls the Canaanite woman a dog. In the lecture I asked whether Jesus was "nice" or, for lack of a better word, acting like a "jerk." My student reasoned that since the Bible is the word of God and Jesus is the Word of God and both have "authority," it's unacceptable that I should even entertain the thought that Jesus was being anything other than "nice" in the Matthew 15 story.

What I realized that day is that inerrancy and infallibility are tied together with authority. If God is perfect, Jesus is perfect and the Bible is also perfect and cannot be questioned whatsoever. The question hinges, for me, on whether as Bible readers we are seeking authority or authoritarianism. I think that as a society, we are seeing elements of others thinking they are above questioning. For example, when Christian Cooper, the Black male bird-watcher, asked Amy Cooper to leash her dog, American society saw how the Amy Coopers of the world do not appreciate being confronted and will weaponize their positions against Black people.

Accordingly, the stakes are high when I begin the action of challenging the inerrancy and infallibility of the sacred text. For many of my students, such an action is tantamount to challenging God! I will argue that to question inerrancy or infallibility is not to challenge God or even the biblical text but rather to challenge the White supremacist authoritarianism behind many interpretations of the biblical text.

A Word on "Inspiration" as "God-Breathed"

The reasons why evangelicals and many mainline Protestants highly regard the doctrines of inerrancy and infallibility stem mainly from 2 Timothy 3:16–17: "All scripture is *inspired by God* (*theopneustos*) and is useful for teaching, for reproof, for correction, and for training in righteousness, so that everyone who belongs to God may be proficient, equipped for every good work" (NRSV, emphasis mine). However, what happens when we interrogate what "all scripture" (*graphō*) means? Often, readers take "all scripture" to mean the Old Testament and the New Testament. However, that is probably not the case, since 2 Timothy 3:16 was written before the texts of the New Testament were formalized as the measuring rod for salvation in the late fourth century. Most likely, the writer of 2 Timothy was thinking about the Torah, the

Prophets, and the Writings of Judaism. Taking our Bible seriously means taking the context of the writers seriously as well.

So how am I reimagining "God-breathed" in this book? Specifically, I am playing with the idea of "God-breathed" in relation to the words "I can't breathe," uttered by both Eric Garner and George Floyd in their final moments and taken up as a slogan of the Black Lives Matter movement. My loose translation of 2 Timothy 3:16–17 is as follows:

> All writings are God-breathed and advantageous toward teaching, toward rebuke, toward correcting faults, toward instruction in justice, so that the person of God may be capable of finishing all good works.[5]

The writer of 2 Timothy suggests that God's breath in the biblical text is advantageous toward a desired end. I translate the Greek preposition *pros* as "toward" to stress the continued movement God's breath compels us to. And I specifically use the term "justice" as opposed to "righteousness" to prod readers toward an idea of faith-based social justice that is inherent even in our ideas of individual righteousness and salvation. The underlying theme of this book is that our faith communities cannot fully breathe because White supremacist authoritarianism in the doctrines of inerrancy and infallibility have stifled God's breath in us.

The Plan of the Book

In chapter 1 I acknowledge my training in Eurocentric biblical interpretation at institutions that, in actuality, attempted to train me

5. The English Standard Version highlights the gendered nature of God's servant: "All Scripture is breathed out by God and profitable for teaching, for reproof, for correction, and for training in righteousness, that the man of God may be complete, equipped for every good work."

to act as a White male biblical scholar. I then move in chapter 2 to uncover White supremacist authoritarianism's connection to the doctrines referred to as the inerrancy and infallibility of Scripture, in essence arguing that White supremacist thought becomes equated with biblical authoritarianism. In chapter 3 I argue that those doctrines can become weapons of structural gaslighting in evangelical and mainline Protestant circles. I reflect on how Black and minoritized bodies attempt to contort themselves to fit within evangelicalism, usually without success. The constant contortion results in the continued loss of breath for Black Christians, as many of us are very aware of wearing masks of White supremacy in our evangelical, Protestant, predominantly White institutions.

Moving on from structural gaslighting, chapter 4 is my attempt to apply Womanist biblical interpretation to a particular text as an example of how White supremacist authoritarianism can be decentered. I ponder mature faith formation by expanding the doctrinal idea of "faith in Jesus Christ" to "walking in the faith of Jesus Christ" unto death (that is, social death to White supremacist authoritarianism in faith communities). To conclude, I consider how mature faith re-members the detrimental ideas of White supremacist authoritarianism *while also* re-membering faith communities.

* * *

As you read this book, I hope you get a sense of my affection for and trust of the sacred text even as I combine that affection and trust with critical thinking. Memoir and scholarship come together here as I seek to build a mature faith and to exorcise the demons of White supremacist authoritarianism.

As we journey toward that goal, I hope to model a type of biblical reading that acknowledges the tension both within the text and in the ways we read it. But as critical as this book is, I hope it is also constructive. I am committed to ethical and holistic biblical interpretation for the liberation of all people—not Black, not White, not generic people of color, but *all people*. White supremacist authoritarianism by way of one-sided doctrines of inerrancy and infallibility distorts our understanding of the way a Christian community should act before God and one another. Such doctrines hinder the proper exercise of the Bible's authority, and that is what this book fights against. Let the work begin.

Chapter 1

STIFLED BREATHING: TRAINED TO BE
A WHITE MALE BIBLICAL SCHOLAR

E very year in November (pre–COVID era) I would attend the
Society of Biblical Literature's Annual Meeting with approx-
imately nine thousand of my friends and colleagues in the field
of biblical studies. What is always interesting about the Annual
Meeting is the sheer number of bodies that can converge upon one
city for five days of conferencing. I remember my first time attend-
ing as a graduate student in 2009. The city was New Orleans, and
I was able to room for two nights with my favorite Hebrew Bible
professor, Ellen Davis.

As an African American female graduate student in a master's
program, I did not have any ties to the already-connected groups
of African American, Hispanic, or Asian American doctoral students within the academy. I felt my first feelings of being adrift
as I navigated conference rooms, meeting halls, and book tables
alone. And what really astounded me was the number of people
who did not look like me. I could walk into a room of hundreds
of people and be the only Black or Brown face in there. White
male scholars are what most of us are used to seeing in various
positions across these United States of America, and when I look
back on my academic training, I am forced to acknowledge that
the bulk of it was trying to prepare me to act as a White male
biblical scholar.

Racial and Gender Dynamics in My Seminary Experience

I'm not sure why I was so surprised by the magnitude of White people at my field's flagship conference. I experienced the same thing in many of my classes at Duke Divinity School. I lobbied twice to be "allowed" into classes taught by Drs. Joel Marcus and Richard Hays but was rebuffed twice because they were "advanced" classes, and apparently I was not advanced enough. I do not remember Dr. Marcus's class title, but the title of Dr. Hays's class remains seared in my brain: "The Old Testament in the New Testament." Oh, how I wanted to take that class. I will never forget the time I peeped in on the class proceedings one day, just to see who was there. I was shocked to find there were only White-looking folks in the class and often wondered what my Black body would have felt and experienced if I had been permitted to join.

I got to find out in different classes with these professors, as I took "Greek Exegesis of the Gospel of Matthew" with Dr. Marcus and "Greek Exegesis of 1 Corinthians" with Dr. Hays in spring 2010. In both, I was the only African American and the only woman. Why do I recall these experiences? Because they were the beginning of professors training me to read as a White male biblical scholar.

Specifically, during a group discussion one day someone mentioned "feeding" parishioners, and I wondered aloud what we as ministers *receive* from those we serve. I remember my colleagues, many of whom would go on in life to be productive and caring United Methodist pastors, pushing back about receiving anything from parishioners. The mentality was that ministers do not receive from their congregants—nor from the poor folks in the neighborhood to whom they may distribute canned goods. No, ministers give and receive nothing back from congregants and neighborhood members. I specifically remember thinking that I am always ministered to when I least expect it, even as I am ministering. Most assuredly, I was reading Paul correctly when I remarked on mutuality in ministry. But I realized my colleagues did not necessarily see the same ideas in Paul. Was it my race or my gender that made me ask these questions, that made me see differently in the Corinthians text? I continue to ponder these questions years later as I teach my own seminary classes.

Specialized Training in Crap No One Cares About

What I experienced at Duke Divinity School were the abstract and heady ways in which many of my colleagues in the classroom engaged the biblical text. I remember specifically a class where we were discussing 1 Corinthians and the progression of the Jesus movement from particularized Judaism to a "universal" religion. Such scholarship stems from the work of Ferdinand Christian Baur (1792–1860), a church historian and theologian who argued that early Christianity was a Hegelian synthesis of Jewish (Petrine) Christianity and Gentile (Pauline) Christianity. At the time I did not understand (nor particularly care) why the work of Baur is important for New Testament studies. Since discovering Womanism as an undergraduate student, I have had difficulty thinking in abstract terms that are set apart from lived experiences. In my mind, Baur is apart from lived experience and cannot speak to the Black church tradition. How would I even engage Baur in a church setting? Oftentimes I think that some of my seminary experiences were specialized training in crap no one cares about.

The work of scholars such as David Horrell and Shawn Kelley comes to mind as I write these words.[1] In my Gospels classes, we would often debate the Jesus of history versus the Jesus of faith.

1. David G. Horrell, *Ethnicity and Inclusion: Religion, Race, and Whiteness in Constructions of Jewish and Christian Identities* (Grand Rapids: Eerdmans, 2020), and Shawn Kelley, *Racializing Jesus: Race, Ideology and the Formation of Modern Biblical Scholarship* (New York: Routledge, 2002), 47.

When I entered seminary, I had a difficult time wrapping my head around historical Jesus studies—and truth be told, sometimes I still do! However, what scholars of Jesus and the historical Jesus find is that language centered on the Jesus of history and on the glorified Jesus actually convey ideas rooted in ethnic identities and nationalism, doing harm to those who do not possess Aryan lineage or come from a White Anglo-Saxon Protestant background. Baur was under the influence of German idealists like G. W. F. Hegel, who believed there was a pure, authentic culture that could be found not only within the biblical text but also in Europe.

Hegel understood the history of the world through the lens of progress. For Hegel, a pure, authentic culture is a culture that progresses toward consciousness of freedom. He believed the "Spirit" directed history through phases, beginning with "the Oriental World," then moving into the Greek and Roman worlds, and finally culminating in the "Germanic" age with Christianity. Both Horrell and Kelly stress that Hegel's philosophy of history and progress is a racialized one that promotes a narrative of western European (specifically German) cultural, religious, and racial superiority.[2] Other cultures (whether Jewish, Black, Asian, etc.), by default, cannot exert such a superiority. Purity and superiority were extended from western European culture to White people themselves, who felt it their duty to expel the racially "alien" (the Jew, the "Oriental," the African, the non-European) from multiple areas of knowledge and from the narrative of world history.[3]

Moreover, as nationalism arose in European academic thinking, the Hegelian logic of moving from lower to higher levels of consciousness began to take root. Hegel espoused consciousness as developing geographically and racially, assigning levels of consciousness to particular races and peoples. For Hegel, lower levels

2. Horrell, *Ethnicity and Inclusion*, 4–5.
3. Kelley, *Racializing Jesus*, 47–50.

of consciousness belong to lesser, backward cultures. On the other hand, Europeans, particularly Germans, are capable of higher levels of consciousness. It is the Germanic Europeans who possess the potential for authentic culture and real freedom. Hegel developed a narrative of history that denied humanity to Africans and denied the consciousness of freedom to Jews and "Orientals."

As I think about my training in asking the "right" questions about the biblical text, I realize that asking proper questions was connected to how the professors who were training me were steeped in Western thought that considered anything "other" as alien or corrupt. So when I asked questions about lived experience related to my identity as an African American woman, my questions needed to be expelled from the classroom setting. In essence, my professors wanted me to learn European philosophical thought so that I could continue to ask questions of the biblical text from a European philosophical viewpoint.

Turning Crap into Womanist Bursts of Air

I did not realize at the time that taking classes on the apostle Paul would actually be a source of transformation of proverbial lead into gold. Many courses on Pauline literature have been relegated to pondering issues of justification and righteousness and what they mean for salvation purposes. What I came to see in my Pauline classes was that even if my professors did not want to allow me the imagination to ask different questions of Paul than what they were attempting to force upon me, there were actually others who may have thought of similar questions to mine but never thought to ask them in ways that I began to formulate.

The inability to give full-throated voice to your own questions based on lived experience is what I characterize as "stifled breath." And I believe that transformation from stifled breath to full Womanist breath is important. So, like the medieval alchemists who sought to make gold out of lead, I am seeking to transform interpretations of Paul from oppressive to liberating, especially for women.

In 2018 it was a surreal moment when the *Journal for Feminist Studies in Religion* notified me that I would receive the second-place Elisabeth Schüssler Fiorenza New Scholars Award, given annually to early-career scholars whose research and insights will shape the future of feminist studies in religion. What I had not realized at the time was that for me to ask new questions of Pauline literature, specifically questions related to the bodies of enslaved Black women in the colonial United States and their relationship to Paul's metaphorical use of slavery language, would actually provide avenues of liberation for actual women in contemporary churches.

As I lecture in various venues, I receive interesting and sometimes disheartening feedback on my readings of Paul. Specifically, I remember a gentleman taking issue with my questioning Paul's language in Galatians and subsequently asking me what I would advise Paul to say today. As I ponder that question, I think I would say to Paul what I say to any man who uncritically uses the bodies of women to make a point: STOP! There is something divine in the ability to tell someone to stop, whether it be Paul himself or a male pastor who arrogates power to himself in the name of Paul. My conversations with women after such lectures are often transformative for me.

Women often see themselves as second-class citizens. Yes, we may serve meals, take care of children, and teach women's Bible studies, but all these duties are usually subsumed under the authority of male headship. Alchemy occurs when women begin to breathe in larger bursts of air instead of constantly holding their breaths because some man (Paul or Pastor) has not allowed full breathing.

From *Stifled Breath* to *Full-Breathed Authority*

As I think about my time learning specialized crap no one cares about in the form of European philosophical thought and its relationship to biblical studies, I realize I actually had to care about it because it stifled my breath. I also began to realize that these ideas around "pure" culture and the subordination of women in leadership were stifling not only my breath but also that of the students I was coming into contact with during my first few years of seminary teaching.

White male biblical scholarship is linked to the idea of objectivity in the academic study of the Bible. For generations biblical scholars studied under the belief that "objective" inquiry was the prime way to do biblical scholarship—that is, keeping one's personal thoughts and feelings away from any inquiry into the biblical text. Objective reality as a stance for biblical interpretation is, I argue, one of the systemic evils of academic biblical studies. Renita Weems begins her seminal article on Womanist hermeneutics by stating that scholarship is now beginning to assert the "inherent biases and limitation of the historical-critical method as an objective, scientific approach to the Bible."[4]

I call stifled breath in the form of objectivity "evil" because I, as a Black woman in biblical studies, was not being trained to be my fully authentic, God-ordained self. Actively engaging issues of identity to confront objectivity in biblical interpretation has helped me "catch my breath" as I construct ways and means of reading biblical texts that are relevant in the halls of the academy, in the pulpits of churches, and on the sidewalks of society

---

4. See Renita Weems, "Womanist Reflections on Biblical Hermeneutics," in *Black Theology: A Documentary History*, ed. James H. Cone and Gayraud S. Wilmore, vol. 2, *1980–1992* (Maryknoll, NY: Orbis, 1993), 216–24.

where lived experience occurs. Relationship across identity lines is important in this task. I contend that a turn to identity coupled with relationality can help us all begin to breathe. My Womanist identity is important to my particular constructive process that aims to transform stifled breath into full embodied breathing in regard to engaging the biblical text.

Fully Breathed Womanist Identity

Linda Martin Alcoff defines identities as "embodied horizons from which we each must confront and negotiate our shared world and specific life condition."[5] These embodied horizons reflect the historical asymmetries of power and well-being that inhere in the categories of race, gender, sexuality, and class. The starting point for my understanding of Womanist identity is consciousness of these felt and lived inequities as well as determination to disrupt them. In her pioneering article "The Black Feminist Consciousness," Katie Geneva Cannon states that a Black feminist consciousness reads the Scriptures in order to struggle for human dignity, fight against White hypocrisy, and wrestle for justice by understanding the prophetic tradition within Scripture as a way to face formidable oppression.[6] I would add to Cannon's formulation the Womanist critique of racist White feminism and a commitment to the well-being of all persons who are racialized, and/or who identify, as Black. Alice Walker coined the term "Womanism" to signal this felt connection to the Black community that seeks to uplift women and men.[7] African American ethicists and theo-

5. Linda Martin Alcoff, *Visible Identities: Race, Gender, and the Self* (New York: Oxford University Press, 2006), 288–89.

6. Katie Geneva Cannon, "The Emergence of Black Feminist Consciousness," in *Feminist Interpretation of the Bible*, ed. Letty M. Russell (Philadelphia: Westminster, 1985), 30–40.

7. Alice Walker, *In Search of Our Mothers' Gardens* (New York: Harcourt Brace Jovanovich, 1967), xi.

logians utilized Walker's theory in church communities and the academy as a way of affirming the identity of African American women as Black while also connecting them with the pioneering work of feminism.[8]

In her work, Walker articulates four tenets of Womanism: radical subjectivity, traditional communalism, redemptive self-love, and critical engagement. Radical subjectivity is the epistemological privileging of Black women's identity and selfhood. It stems from the African folk expression "You actin' womanish." Black mothers would often say this to their Black daughters whenever the daughter acted as though she knew too much. Traditional communalism is the recognition of the collective value of the entire Black community. If a slave was going to walk to Canada to gain her freedom, she was not going alone; she was taking everyone else with her. Redemptive self-love is love and acceptance of the self regardless of what others say or think. When a Womanist proposes redemptive self-love, she recognizes that there is a struggle that occurs within herself and with other people as she seeks and asserts her desire for self-love. A Womanist loves the struggle because it means there is room for growth and that she has neither given up on life nor yielded to the struggle. Finally, critical engagement is a deep and sustained analysis of Jacquelyn Grant's tridimensional intersection of oppression: racism, sexism, and classism. Critical engagement also includes dialogue with feminism since Womanists recognize that "Womanist is to feminist as purple is to lavender," meaning that Womanist purple is a deeper shade of feminist lavender.[9]

---

8. For the impact of Womanism on theology and religious studies, see Delores S. Williams, *Sisters in the Wilderness: The Challenge of Womanist God-Talk* (Maryknoll, NY: Orbis, 2013); Stephanie Y. Mitchem, *Introducing Womanist Theology* (Maryknoll, NY: Orbis, 2006); and Stacy M. Floyd-Thomas, ed., *Deeper Shades of Womanism in Religion and Society* (New York: New York University Press, 2006).

9. Walker, *In Search of Our Mothers' Gardens*, xii.

For Womanists, identity is also connected to the body.[10] I've been forced to ask where my body can stand that actually makes predominantly White institutions feel good about themselves. In this thought I agree with M. Shawn Copeland, who notes that the "Black woman's body has been reduced to body parts—parts that allowed white men pleasure, however unsettling; parts that afforded white men economic gain; parts that literally nursed the heirs of White racist supremacy."[11] Part of recognizing my own identity as a Black woman in the United States is recognizing that Black women's bodies have stood at the oppressing intersection of gender, race/ethnicity, class, colonialism, and sexuality for hundreds of years.

Scholars such as Kelly Brown Douglas make the connection between Black women's bodies and the development of colonial slavery in the United States, noting that Black women often become the quintessential example of the so-called Black Jezebel: "Black females were bought and sold according to their reproductive capacity."[12] By distorting Black women's sexuality, the Jezebel image "protected the White Slavocracy and fostered the exercise of tyrannical White power."[13] White male masters could play the victim, since they were seduced by their enslaved Black Jezebels. They exhibited what we now call "victim blaming."[14] As

10. See especially Kelly Brown Douglas, *What's Faith Got to Do with It? Black Bodies/Christian Souls* (Maryknoll, NY: Orbis, 2005); and M. Shawn Copeland, *Enfleshing Freedom: Body, Race, and Being* (Minneapolis: Fortress, 2008).

11. See M. Shawn Copeland, "Body, Representation, and Black Religious Discourse," in *Womanist Theological Ethics: A Reader*, ed. Katie Geneva Cannon, Emilie M. Townes, and Angela D. Sims (Louisville: Westminster John Knox, 2011), 98–112.

12. Kelly Brown Douglas, *Sexuality and the Black Church* (Maryknoll, NY: Orbis, 1999), 40.

13. Douglas, *Sexuality and the Black Church*, 40.

14. Legal studies recognize victim blaming as a devaluing act where the victim of a crime, an accident, or any type of abusive maltreatment is

a result of slavery, Black female sexuality has been a seen/unseen dilemma. Cultural tropes portray Black female sexuality as hyper-active and lucrative for pornographic consumption, and thus Black women often hide their sexuality in order to divert an unwanted pornographic gaze.[15]

Douglas goes further in her work by connecting the devalua-tion of Black bodies to developments in Christian theology and theology's relationship to Black female sexuality. As she sees it, Black bodies undergo "redemptive suffering" in order to become "white souls."[16] Engaging Augustine of Hippo's thoughts on sexu-ality and his use of Paul's writings, Douglas shows that Augustine was a "major conduit" of dualistic, Platonized Christianity into the Western theological tradition. Augustine's eventual disavowal of bodily pleasure led to later theological constructions of a hier-archy of spirit over body, men over women, Christian over non-Christian, and eventually White over Black. Douglas shows Chris-tianity's complicity in maligning Black bodies, especially during times of lynching in the Jim/Jane Crow South, where Black bodies were often abducted and killed after Whites convened for church. Specifically, Douglas shows that Augustinian ideals prompted Black women to deny the fullness of their sexuality and of their bodies in order to gain spiritual redemption.[17] In the next chapter

---

held as wholly or partially responsible for the wrongful conduct commit-ted against them. Victim blaming can appear in the form of negative social reactions from legal, medical, and mental health professionals, as well as from the media and immediate family members and other acquaintances. Traditionally, victim blaming has emerged in racist and sexist forms. The reason for victim blaming can be attributed to misconceptions about vic-tims, perpetrators, and the nature of violent acts. See "Victim Blaming," http://definitions.uslegal.com/v/victim-blaming/.

15. See Tamura Lomax, *Jezebel Unhinged: Loosing the Black Female Body in Religion and Culture* (Durham, NC: Duke University Press, 2008).

16. Kelly Brown Douglas, *Stand Your Ground: Black Bodies and the Justice of God* (Maryknoll, NY: Orbis, 2015), 35.

17. Douglas, *What's Faith*, 175.

I will make the connection between denying one's body and the doctrines that enable White supremacist authoritarianism.

Because of the influence of Augustine, part of Black biblical hermeneutics has meant not problematizing Paul's language in his epistles. However, in chapter 4 I will engage my own Womanist identity in conversation with Paul's language of "faith" in Galatians to argue that the doctrines of inerrancy and infallibility have stifled the breathing ability of Womanists as we read Pauline literature.

This is where ideas of who has the authority to ask certain questions of Scripture come to the forefront. In the next chapter I will show how some of these questions come into play in regard to my own embodied identity and how folks begin to construct lenses for reading the Bible without connection to their embodied identities. I will argue that White Supremacist authoritarianism is devoid of connection to identity. For my particular Womanist hermeneutic, reading the biblical text means integrating the traditional historical-critical practices of biblical scholarship with the real lived experiences of Black women. What I suggest in my ongoing work in the academy, in faith-based settings, and in society is a reading of the biblical text in mutuality with Black women's lived experience, Black women's reasoning, and some element of Black church tradition in order to construct a Womanist biblical methodology that undermines objectivity in biblical scholarship.[18]

---

18. Even though recent work on Womanist biblical interpretation states that African American women have made minimal impact on biblical scholarship (see Nyasha Junior's *An Introduction to Womanist Biblical Interpretation* [Louisville: Westminster John Knox, 2015], 121), there are actually a number of self-identified Womanists who perform biblical interpretation and who have made an impact on biblical scholarship within the past twenty-five years. I argue that continued crossover between theology and biblical studies will make a huge impact on both fields.

Questions for Consideration

Have you ever been told to not ask certain questions of the biblical text? If so, what do those memories stir up within you?

Have you ever read a biblical text and wondered where your body would be in the story? If so, what were some of your thoughts? If not, can you begin to imagine how the biblical text "feels" to someone who cannot imagine where their body is in the story?

Has your own identity been disparaged through others' reading of the Bible in such a way that you have never wanted to read the Bible again?

Chapter 2

White Supremacist Authoritarianism
Is Not God's Breath

I n this chapter I will connect White supremacist authoritarianism to the doctrinal teachings understood as the "inerrancy" and "infallibility" of Scripture and to strategies promoted by various people (mostly men) in power. As mentioned in the introduction, by "White supremacist authoritarianism" I mean the problematic and misguided use of authority based on an ideology steeped in White supremacy.

Defining Biblical Authority

Auctoritas

As I am sure you have already surmised, I have not become a White male biblical scholar. And my doctoral adviser, Seung Ai Yang, is responsible for not letting such a becoming occur! I invoke the name of my now-retired doctoral adviser to highlight how the idea of authority has shifted in my thinking about the biblical text.

In her work, Yang begins to unpack the idea of authority as she considers her Catholic and Buddhist upbringing. The English word "authority" descends from the Latin word *auctoritas*, which functioned very differently in Roman society than it did in her Korean Catholic-Buddhist context.[1]

1. See Seung Ai Yang, "The Word of Creative Love, Peace, and Justice,"

In Roman imperial society, *auctoritas* is distinct from the word "imperial"[2] (derived from *imperium*), which connotes the idea of rights held by government officials. In contrast, *auctoritas* allows for the interpretation of and elaboration upon the wisdom of those who came before. As Old Testament scholar William Brown notes, *auctoritas* is more creative. While precedent does matter when it comes to *auctoritas*, what matters more is having conversations with what comes before and after. Therefore, the idea of authority actually stems from movement between interpretation and contextualization. What would our faith communities look like if we fully embraced an idea of biblical authority that lives and breathes in such a movement? If we embraced the need for an abiding sense of connection to what has happened in the past while having continued conversation with our present and imagining what future conversations could entail?

"Preaching to" versus "Conversations with"

I regard authority as a "living" and "breathing" conversation. However, what many of us fail to understand is that conversation is always mutual. Has the idea of the "preaching" hour replaced the concept of conversation as we think about biblical authority? How is the idea of Bible study, where congregants come and reason together about biblical texts, related to preaching moments? In essence, I am pondering how the act of "preaching to" has shifted many congregants away from "conversations with" pastors and even with the biblical text.

If we understand authority to be conversational, then how do

---

in *Engaging Biblical Authority: Perspectives on the Bible as Scripture*, ed. William P. Brown (Louisville: Westminster John Knox, 2007). Three essays in this volume—by personal mentors Seung Ai Yang and Ellen F. Davis and by Womanist hero Katie Geneva Cannon—have been particularly helpful for my thinking over the years.

2. See Brown's introduction in *Engaging Biblical Authority*.

we embark on authoritative conversations with the biblical text? I would argue that thinking through the concept of authority is where the act of "breathing" becomes even more important. Conversations, like relationships, should be generative and transformative. They demand response and mutuality. Relationships shape who we are and form our identity in most instances. I am daughter to Robert and Argie and wife to Victor and mother to Ebony and Saron. However, all these relationships change, ebb, and flow. Even as I remain Robert and Argie's daughter, I have grown into an adult woman. No longer do Robert and Argie make all my decisions, as they did when I was a child. The relationship transforms. The same goes for my relationship with Ebony and Saron. Why do we want to fix in eternal space our relationship to the Bible and to God? Neither relationships nor conversations remain fixed!

Some level of fluidity is required, even though most evangelicals would understand biblical authority to be fixed. Fixedness perpetually keeps parish members as immature children in relationship to the Bible and to God, as does "preaching to." If we take biblical authority seriously, then we also have to take seriously the Bible's ability to transform each and every one of us from immature to mature communities of faith and from immature to mature conversation partners. White supremacist thought in the midst of biblical authority is immature and promotes immature readings of and conversations with the biblical text.

So where does maturity originate? If we truly believe the biblical text is not equivalent to God but mediates God's presence, then we also have to take into account the diversity of contexts, authors, cultures, and worldviews of every person who wrote portions of what the church has canonized as Scripture. The ability to discern the many voices within the biblical text is the challenging task of mature biblical interpretation. Mature people engage the complexity of the biblical text as it points us to the presence of God without it becoming God or an idol.

Moving from Bibliolatry to Inspired Biblical Authority

In my classes I advise students to buy the quick and cheap *Pocket Dictionary of Biblical Studies*, and I alert them to one of the terms inside: "bibliolatry." Bibliolatry is a pejorative term used to describe the practice of focusing so much attention on the Bible *as a book to be venerated and idolized in itself* that the fact that it is divine revelation from God transmitted through human authors is overlooked.[3] I argue even further that bibliolatry also obscures other important issues, including the intricacies of "faith."

One example I offer to students is that I love my husband immensely and deeply. That does not mean we never experience tense moments in our relationship. Earlier in my life I would have blindly accepted his counsel regarding all areas of my life since I, like many evangelicals, believed that the husband is the head of and final authority over the wife. To be honest, moving from a mindset of unquestioned obedience to my spouse to having mature conversations with him wherein I sometimes accept and sometimes reject his counsel has allowed me to move from unquestioned obedience to a text to mature conversation with a text. Hear me well: I love my husband, and he is an authority in my life. He is not *the* authority in my life, though. I also love the biblical text, and it is an authority in my life but not *the* authority in my life.

As a practicing Buddhist *and* Catholic, my doctoral adviser Seung Ai Yang often regaled us students with stories from the Buddhist tradition that were spot-on as we engaged biblical interpretation and issues of authority. One such story tells of a Buddhist teacher who takes his students up to the top of a mountain. He then points toward the moon and tells the students to identify

---

3. A. G. Patzia and A. J. Petrotta, *Pocket Dictionary of Biblical Studies* (Downers Grove, IL: InterVarsity, 2002), 21.

and ponder that to which he is pointing. As the students focus on their teacher's finger, the teacher advises that they focus not on the finger but on that to which the finger points. The biblical text is the finger that points to the almighty God.

What Yang's story taught me is that I grew up as a bibliolater. A bibliolater is a person who practices bibliolatry—that is, one who treats the Bible as equivalent to God. One who, effectively, worships it as an idol. Yes, we may accept the Bible as guidance for our rule of faith, but what happens when our view of the Bible moves from reasonable reverence to irrational reverence? Irrational reverence means folks begin to use the Bible not as a conversation starter but as a conversation ender. Think of the phrase "the Bible says" and how it is often considered the be-all and end-all in an argument. The biblical text becomes a bludgeoning tool used to exert supremacist authoritarianism; what the Bible says (or rather, how the wielder interprets what the Bible says) goes. My argument is that irrational reverence of the Bible is often a form of *White* supremacist authoritarianism, because it is usually White men who have wielded the power of the Bible.

We did not get to the point of irrational reverence without doctrines that are meant as a guardrail to keep our questions and interpretations from running off the road. Those doctrines are inerrancy and infallibility. Accordingly, we must ask: Where does the Bible's authority come from? Do we look to the literal words on the page of an English translation? Does authority come from the biblical text's connection to "apostolic witness"? Is some combination at play? Or perhaps the biblical text's authority comes from the whisper of the Holy Spirit that often points to the words' impact and importance? I believe the latter: that biblical authority, as opposed to White supremacist authoritarianism, comes from the small whisper of the female Holy Spirit[4] that prompts and prods

---

4. I intentionally play with "Spirit" as feminine. In ancient languages,

divine understandings of ourselves even as we negotiate our relationship with the Almighty.

Katie Cannon shows how African American professors depart from the "normative" (read "White male") assumptions in our various guilds to bring a radical critique to inherited Eurocentric traditions and kerygmatic assertions that minimize Black people's actualization of our God-given authenticity.[5] I go beyond Cannon by arguing that inherited Eurocentric traditions around the biblical text, such as doctrines of inerrancy and infallibility, actually minimize Black people's ability to exert our God-given, inspired breath—our authority. Part of my job in this book is to develop a genuine understanding of biblical authority, apart from White supremacist authoritarianism, that will foster a healthy society in which all participants are able to make distinctive and valuable contributions and therefore *BREATHE!*

Starting with the Bible as the bearer of authority, we can say that women and Black and minoritized bodies may benefit from what the Bible has to share. The narrative structure of the Bible allows women and men to see God's involvement in the world to offer us salvation—that is, fullness of life—through faith in, and because of the faith of, Jesus the Christ.[6]

As I think about the year 2020 and what living in an unhealthy society has done to human flourishing in the United States (my present context), I see that part of what many experience is some parties having and exercising authority while other parties do not, thus allowing authoritarianism to slip into society as a norm. Once

---

words do not signify biology, but they are designated as masculine, feminine, or neuter. The Hebrew word for spirit, *ruach*, is morphologically a feminine word. The Greek word for spirit, *pneuma*, is morphologically neuter.

5. See Katie G. Cannon, "The Biblical Mainstay of Liberation," in *Engaging Biblical Authority*.

6. I will offer my particular Womanist interpretation and translation of the "faith in Christ" and "faith of Christ" constructions in chapter 4.

White supremacist authoritarianism became the norm in society, we slipped from genuine authority to authoritarianism. The problem we will face (and probably not solve) is identifying exactly when such authoritarianism slipped in, both in society and in our readings of the biblical text through the doctrines of inerrancy and infallibility.[7] Regardless, there are definitive psychological ways in which these ideas have played out, both politically (in the form of the Southern Strategy) and religiously (in the form of protective strategies in evangelical thought).

Strategies as a Means of Control

As I was preparing to write this book, I had to plan out my strategy. I had to strategize around my own experience and training in biblical scholarship in order to craft an argument and articulate it in the best ways possible. In putting together this small book, I exerted control over my strategy.

Strategy, however, can work in other ways. I am trying to strategize in order to succeed in a particular argument. There are others in society who strategize for control and power that place one group of people over another group of people. I would argue that the Southern Strategy (an electoral scheme that I will discuss later in this chapter) and "protective strategies" in evangelical thought are operating in similar ways and with similar effects. Here is my argument in a nutshell: Because the doctrines of inerrancy and infallibility are designed to protect the idea of Scripture being free from

---

7. Scholars are highlighting how, when, and where White supremacy codified itself as part of religion. See, for example, Eric P. Weed, *The Religion of White Supremacy in the United States* (Lanham, MD: Lexington Books, 2017). Weed explores in-depth legal cases, slave codes before Reconstruction, laws after Reconstruction, and the reemergence of White supremacy at the election of Donald J. Trump.

error and from failing to accomplish its predetermined purpose, they act as tools of control for the people who normally have the most power over deciding the "proper" readings of Scripture. These people tend to be a certain group: White male biblical scholars.

So what do these doctrines actually control? According to my research, these doctrines control the questions one can ask of the biblical text. The questions I had of Jesus's encounter with the Canaanite woman, for example, are deemed heretical, and not asking them places me in the box I'm supposed to want to be in: the box of White male biblical scholar. The doctrines of biblical inerrancy and infallibility further exude power by becoming protective strategies around the biblical text itself.

Doctrine as a Powerful Protective Strategy

As I have recently moved from the Pacific Northwest to Georgia, my thought processes have shifted slightly as my body has returned to a southern state. Now as I teach in a Baptist-affiliated theological institution, I am constantly thinking through how issues surrounding the Baptist denomination impact my thinking around issues such as doctrines and their power. My current institutional home was founded as a result of a grand exodus from the Southern Baptist Convention and the more conservative Southern Baptist seminaries. Many of my colleagues have experienced the trauma of once identifying with a denomination that holds the biblical text as both inerrant and infallible. When these colleagues could no longer hold to a complementarian idea of marriage nor accept the ineligibility of women for ordination or even for teaching in a seminary context, they joined the more moderate Cooperative Baptist Fellowship and my current institutional home.

In essence, the Southern Baptist Convention had created what scholars such as Wayne Proudfoot call a protective strategy around the twin doctrines of inerrancy and infallibility (as my good friend Stephen Young pointed out to me in his own fine essay).[8] Protective strategies are simply ways in which particular interpreters privilege certain religious claims and then seal them off from any type of academic analysis. Any terms, beliefs, and judgments must concur and meet with that interpreter's approval. This is a protective strategy. In other words, White male biblical scholars have outlined inerrancy and infallibility in such a way that anyone who questions or pushes back against these accepted viewpoints becomes disciplined and subsequently ostracized. Young (among other scholars) mentions, for example, the excommunication of Robert H. Gundry from the Evangelical Theological Society.

In 1982 Gundry's commentary on the Gospel of Matthew was published. In it he argues that the Gospel writer intentionally employed midrash, altering and embellishing the account of the birth of Jesus by adding magi and a star. Rabbinic midrash is an exegetical approach that seeks to discern value in the biblical texts by reimagining dominant readings while also formulating news ones to stand alongside. Midrash is comfortable with not providing answers, leaving readers to answer questions on their own. As a cultural way of reading, rabbinic midrash does not adhere to one meaning alone that stems from the biblical text; there may be a variety of readings. I would argue that Christian fundamentalism is uncomfortable with various interpretations and readings standing alongside others. In fact, part of authoritarian thought is the idea that every biblical passage has only one right interpretation and that all passages across all the biblical books must be perfectly harmonized. Disagreement among biblical authors or interpreters is not valued—quite the opposite.

8. See Stephen L. Young, "Protective Strategies and the Prestige of the 'Academic': A Religious Studies and Practice Theory Re-description of Evangelical Inerrantist Scholarship," *Biblical Interpretation* 23 (2015): 1–35.

Gundry argues that the Matthean writer was teaching about Jesus as the Christ while doing so with factually inadequate material. Specifically, he claims that the Matthean writer substituted the magi, who are not historical, in Matthew 2:1–12 for the shepherds in Luke 2:8–15 in order to lead up to the star, thus replacing the angels and the heavenly host.[9] In the rational thought of the Evangelical Theological Society, Gundry's view that the Matthean writer uses "nonfactual" midrash to prove a theological point (Jesus as the Star of David and the royal Messiah) undermined the inerrancy of Scripture. Further, Gundry does not harmonize Matthew's Gospel with Luke's, meaning he doesn't insist that Jesus's infancy included all the characters and events outlined in each Gospel. Thus Gundry was forced to resign, and the protective strategy around inerrancy and infallibility was solidified.

Why is the story of Gundry's expulsion from the Evangelical Theological Society relevant? I would argue that these same issues crop up today in our understandings of evangelical conversations. For example, in response to discussions within the Southern Baptist Convention about women preaching, prominent evangelical pastor John MacArthur declared in 2019 that the SBC had moved beyond biblical authority, asserting, "When you literally overturn the teaching of Scripture to empower people who want power, you have given up biblical authority."[10] (The same year, he also told Christian author, speaker, and ministry leader Beth Moore to "go home.") What MacArthur fails to realize is that his own identity has been steeped in power because of his particular view of "bib-

9. Craig D. Allert, *A High View of Scripture? The Authority of the Bible and the Formation of the New Testament Canon* (Grand Rapids: Baker Academic, 2007), 166.

10. Quoted in Morgan Lee, "John MacArthur Is No Stranger to Controversy: A Closer Look at the Ministry and Theology behind the Outspoken California Pastor," *Christianity Today*, October 23, 2019, https://www.christianitytoday.com/ct/2019/october-web-only/john-macarthur-beth-moore-controversy.html.

lical authority," which is not a breathed conversation but a top-down authoritarianism.

And this issue of power is relevant for how some Christians view their lack of power and wanting to obtain power, as they will uphold certain presidential administrations as opposed to other, more liberative administrations. The election of Donald Trump is a worthy example. When then-candidate Donald Trump visited Sioux Center, Iowa, in 2016 to campaign for the presidency, he said to a group of evangelical Christians that "Christianity will have power again."[11] Trump's statement begs the question "What exactly is this 'power'?" As both a woman and an African American in the United States, I have been raised in a Baptist history that excludes my identity. As a woman, I'm disallowed the viable option of preaching the gospel, since "Jesus appointed only men" as apostles. Moreover, as an African American, I have studied intensely how supporting slavery caused a break between Baptists of the North and Baptists of the South. My embodied identity as Black woman stands in tension with those in power who seek to hold on to that power even today.

There is an insistence that disbelief in the doctrines of inerrancy and infallibility regarding the biblical text disavows the church of some of its power. People think that having a "high view of Scripture" means one cannot budge from a literal interpretation in all areas. The fear is that if you budge on one bit, the whole thing begins to fall apart.

For me, this is where my former teacher Ellen Davis's work is extremely relevant. Davis touches on the matters of Scripture, languages, and humility.[12] When MacArthur states that things begin

11. Quoted in Colin Campbell, "Trump: If I'm President, 'Christianity Will Have Power' in the US," *Business Insider*, January 23, 2016, https://www.businessinsider.com/donald-trump-christianity-merry-christmas-2016-1.

12. See Ellen F. Davis, "The Soil That Is Scripture," in *Engaging Biblical Authority*.

to fall apart, I ask: What is so bad about things falling apart? More specifically, what is so catastrophic about things falling apart that were never meant to "be" in the first place? Davis would argue that part of our job as biblical scholars is to engage with the inexhaustible complexity of Scripture. We dig in the soil over and over again. That constant digging means we constantly question, we delve into biblical languages (Hebrew, Aramaic, and Greek), and we recognize our own humility in the midst. Delving into these texts, Davis says, allows for the beginning of critical consciousness that engages varieties within the biblical text. Engagement in critical consciousness is the way faith communities are supposed to talk to one another about our faith commitments as we read diversities within our text.

I would count John MacArthur as a power broker who takes a "one and done" approach to Scripture and who does not till the soil. He has all the answers, knows all the answers, and mediates all the answers to his congregation as a strategy to protect inerrancy and infallibility. But what happens when folks embrace a protective strategy for upholding power at all costs? Womanist biblical scholars such as myself come along with the argument that people in power employ protective strategies in order to keep their power.

Connecting Protective Strategies with the Southern Strategy

There is a reason why the 1983 resignation of Robert Gundry from the Evangelical Theological Society is important. I argue that the strategies to keep people in "evangelical power" are similar to strategies to keep leaders in political power. In particular, I argue that protective strategies and the Southern Strategy share overlapping agendas, histories, and time lines that help me, as a woman trained to be a White male biblical scholar, question how certain biblical doctrines become important.

The Southern Strategy

The "Southern Strategy" is traditionally understood as the Republican Party courting Southern White voters in the wake of the civil rights movement of the 1960s, but in *The Long Southern Strategy*, Angie Maxwell and Todd Shields argue that this idea is oversimplified. The Southern Strategy works so well because it also capitalizes on fears pertaining to feminism and religion, hence providing a particularly poignant backdrop for my understanding of doctrine as a Womanist New Testament scholar. My identity as a woman and an African American who teaches in a religious institution sets up a trifecta of fear factors.

Maxwell and Shields argue that the GOP has, with great success, married ideas about women's place in society, White evangelical Christianity, White racial grievances, and even issues pertaining to the economy. Because the strategy worked only temporarily (until the election of Georgian Southern Baptist Jimmy Carter in 1976), new coded messages had to be spread so that Ronald Reagan could secure his 1980 run for the presidency. Reagan advocated that the United States move past identity and become "color-blind" while also invoking the idea of the "welfare queen," code for a Black woman driving a Cadillac while receiving over $150,000 a year in tax-free entitlements from the government as a result of her twelve social security cards. Reagan's portrait of undeserving racial minorities as "takers" was successful. I would argue that by using language about Mexicans being "rapists and murderers" who are "bringing drugs" in caravans to the United States, the Trump administration utilized the same strategy as Reagan.

The Southern Strategy was not limited to speaking only about racial minorities. Maxwell and Shields say the Southern Strategy advocated for Southern female voters to live up to the ideals of "Southern White womanhood." This construct, which had been manufactured in the antebellum era to justify the South's racial hierarchy, asserted that White women were delicate and fragile and needed constant protection from Black males. Over time it cast White supremacy as chivalry while relegating Southern White women to a pedestal in the home where they could be taken care of by men. As a Womanist New Testament scholar, the bells ringing in my head come from the "household codes" found in our New Testament texts—those rules that govern domestic relationships. These relationships pertain to pairs, such as husbands and wives, parents and children, masters and slaves. The household codes appear in Ephesians 5:18–6:9, Colossians 3:18–4:6, and 1 Peter 2:13–3:7. Curiously, some scholars also identify Romans 13:1–4 as a household code even though pairs do not exist in that text, which would seem to dictate that the government is also a manager of a house that must be obeyed.[13] In the Southern Strategy, Republicans began championing "traditional" gender roles while politicizing abortion and LGBTIQ rights as being associated with feminism.

Maxwell and Shields reveal that these battles morphed into the portrayal of Democrats as a threat to Christian fundamentalism. Thinking back to the Evangelical Theological Society's ousting of Gundry from their membership, we can see that it, too, was triggered by a sense of threat to certain Christian fundamentals—in this case, the inerrancy and infallibility of Scripture. Accordingly, the protective strategies found in the Gundry conversation mirror the Southern Strategy of the Republican political machinery, which aims to "protect" fundamental ideas about culture, women's place, racial issues, and economics that appeal to a particular type of Christian.

The long Southern Strategy has come to fruition and is still working. Southern White evangelicals no longer require a politi-

13. M. S. DeMoss, in *Pocket Dictionary for the Study of New Testament Greek* (Downers Grove, IL: InterVarsity, 2001), 69.

cal candidate who holds authentic Christian beliefs. Maxwell and Shields understand such support as part of the "magic" of Donald Trump's election to the presidency. I was stunned by their statistic that only 25 percent of White women voted for Black Democrat Stacey Abrams in Georgia's 2018 gubernatorial race, preferring instead the White male Republican candidate Brian Kemp. For me, this preference reveals that even if I am a reasoned interpreter of the biblical text, many of you may be more comfortable with a White male biblical scholar if it means that White supremacist authoritarianism keeps my embodied identity in servitude.

What Do These Strategies Mean for "Biblical Authority"?

Both protective strategies and the Southern Strategy, while alluding to some fundamental Christian doctrines, really should be understood in ways that are more culturally and psychologically grounded.

Earlier in this chapter I alluded to the idea of White evangelicals gaining "power" if they elected Donald Trump to the presidency. Scholars such as Craig Allert point out that evangelicals in the United States, when they began to sense that they were gradually losing their cultural hegemony, set up the defensive posture of a particular high view of Scripture as a set of dogmas to be embraced, upheld, and protected at all costs. Allert and others are why I highlight the issue of protective strategies and the Gundry resignation.

One aspect of my doctoral work at Chicago Theological Seminary was that I could not engage the New Testament without a cultural element added to my program. Specifically, my PhD is in "Bible, Culture, and Hermeneutics." While at CTS, Yang exposed me to the work of Marxist thinkers such as Antonio Gramsci. Now hear me well, dear reader! I can already begin to hear the cries and arguments that critical theories have absolutely nothing to do with Christianity or biblical interpretation! Many evangelicals will argue that Christianity and critical theories are mutually exclusive and cannot speak to one another. While I, of course, do not imbibe every drop from the fountain of critical theory, as a thinking New Testament scholar, I appreciate the ways in which I can think critically about the similarities and differences between contemporary society and the society in which Jesus and Paul ministered. Critical theory gives me language to address how certain areas of evangelical thought are organized, using the paradigm and frameworks espoused by some Marxist thinkers.

Returning to Marxist thought, what is interesting about linking Gramsci to the protective strategies of evangelical thought is Gramsci's idea of cultural hegemony as domination of a culturally diverse society by a ruling class. In American evangelicalism, when the ruling "Christian" class sensed their impending loss of cultural hegemony, evangelicals enacted protective strategies as a defensive posture to maintain the boundaries around their core set of dogmas, as scholars like Allert have shown. Evangelicals were now protecting dogmas that were set by the agenda of the battle against theological liberalism and against what would become part of the progressive Christian viewpoint.[14]

When a 2020 Pew Research poll released data showing that about seven in ten White evangelicals say the Bible should influence US laws over the will of the people,[15] I had to ask: Whose reading and interpretations do they espouse? It appears that these evangelicals are hoping, praying, and fasting for a time when they experience the return of a particular cultural hegemonic power that stems from a White supremacist reading of the biblical text.

14. Allert, *High View of Scripture*, 30.
15. "Americans Split on How Much Bible Should Sway Laws," Pew Research Center, Washington, DC (April 10, 2020), https://www.pewresearch .org/fact-tank/2020/04/13/half-of-americans-say-bible-should-influence-u -s-laws-including-28-who-favor-it-over-the-will-of-the-people/.

Again, I would uphold that such readings stem from an idea of the inerrancy and infallibility of the biblical text. Again, I remind you of Donald Trump's promise to grant power to a particular sect of Christianity—namely, White evangelicals.

In conjunction with the idea of maintaining cultural hegemony, it would seem there is a psychological component we must engage as we ponder together the relationship of inerrancy and infallibility to White supremacist authoritarianism and biblical interpretation. Evangelicals have traditionally affirmed the authority of the Bible in their denominational statements, and the tradition continues today. As Brian Malley, a specialist in the psychology of spiritual development, emphasizes, these affirmations and statements of faith distinguish outsiders from insiders and serve as a standard for what teaching is permitted within church association.[16] Boundaries become important for understanding membership in certain evangelical circles.

With that stated, I have to wonder what the ramifications are, psychologically speaking, for desiring to be part of an ecclesial community that has such delineated boundaries. If culture making is an unpacking of some of the cognitive elements required to form a community, what are some of the psychological elements? Specifically, if community members assume shared views about inerrancy and infallibility and what these ideas mean for community formation, what happens if such ideas are detrimental to the identity of some members of the community? I would argue that a certain rationalization has to occur psychologically in order for some members to contort themselves into the mold created by the doctrines of inerrancy and infallibility as tools of White supremacist authoritarianism. And that, dear reader, is the subject of the next chapter!

16. See Brian Malley, *How the Bible Works: An Anthropological Study of Evangelical Biblicism* (New York: AltaMira, 2004). Malley's work is an in-depth human research study on evangelical biblicism. He argues well how the Bible functions in evangelical contexts in the chapter "Biblical Authority."

Questions for Consideration

Take a moment to ponder how you have understood the authority of the Bible. How was that authority explained to you? Who explained the authority of the Bible to you? What did you learn previously that remains with you today about biblical authority?

Strategies of protection are not necessarily negative tools. The following is a theological question beyond the scope of this book, but here it goes: What do strategies of protection actually protect? And who benefits? Does the protective strategy of biblical inerrancy and infallibility really protect the biblical text, or does it serve primarily to keep certain groups in power? If we really wanted to "protect" the Bible or "protect" God (I can't imagine why we would have to if God is all-powerful), how would we go about doing that?

Chapter 3

Stop Gaslighting Me

N ow that we've looked at the ways in which culture and psychology play a role in White supremacist authoritarianism, I will move to a discussion of the doctrines of inerrancy and infallibility as agents of gaslighting. Specifically, I will consider how women and Black and minoritized bodies are conditioned to read Scripture in a particular way that disavows what they may see within the text while also forcing them to wear masks of White supremacy. I will argue that gaslighting through doctrines shaped in particular readings of the biblical text are tools of White Supremacist authoritarianism that seek to promote "godly order" at the expense of the critical-thinking minds of both women and Black and minoritized Christians. Moreover, I will ponder how Black and minoritized bodies contort themselves to fit within "traditional" readings of biblical text without success. Finally, this chapter will end with a "Sankofa" moment in which I display a way of reclaiming biblical interpretation that pushes against the traditional mold.

To ground the chapter, I must begin with basic definitions of important terms: "microaggression" and "gaslighting."

Microaggression That Leads to Blame and Shame

Microaggression is "a relatively minor insulting event made disproportionately harmful by taking part in an oppressive pattern of insults," and it is connected to systemic macroaggressions.[1] In other words, an incident of microaggression is particularly harmful because it works within a larger system of domination and oppression.

First, regarding microaggression, the ways in which scholars understand the insults or slights stem partly from the idea that they are mostly unintentional. Scholars talk about well-intentioned people trying to say or do things they do not understand as coming across as microaggressive. However, regardless of the actual intent of the microaggressor, the microaggressive act still fits within a larger pattern of heteronormative, racist, masculinist, ableist, sexist, transphobic, ageist, etc. structures. Moreover, since microaggression is harm based on and inviting questions of blame, shame follows close behind.

I would argue that since many evangelicals are predisposed to thinking about individual salvation as the paramount idea behind their reading the biblical text as inerrant and infallible, a healthy dose of personal shame is appropriate for conviction unto repentance. However, there are other theoretical frameworks regarding shame that connect to issues of microaggression. Melissa Harris-Perry identifies how Black women in America are conditioned to attempt to "stand straight in a crooked room" by holding on to shame.[2] Cognitive psychologists understand that people try to find the "upright" in their surroundings. The problem is that society grants some folks the opportunity to stand upright no matter what their circumstances entail. Specifically, White supremacist

---

1. Many of the definitions in this chapter come from a recent philosophical work on microaggression: Saba Fatima, "I Know What Happened to Me: The Epistemic Harms of Microaggression," in *Microaggressions and Philosophy*, ed. Lauren Freeman and Jeanine Weekes Schroer (New York: Taylor & Francis Group, 2020), 163–83.

2. Melissa Harris-Perry, *Sister Citizen: Shame, Stereotypes, and Black Women in America* (New Haven: Yale University Press, 2011), 28–50.

authoritarianism allows White identity to stand upright even if it has been (pardon my language) crooked as hell!

For example, I note the "crooked" nature of contemporary politics in the ascension of Associate Justice Amy Coney Barrett to the Supreme Court of the United States. Supreme Court Justice Ruth Bader Ginsburg died September 18, 2020, and, reportedly, her dying wish was for the winner of the 2020 presidential election to appoint her replacement. Famously, there is a precedent for a Supreme Court seat to remain open for a number of months until after a presidential election, established in 2016 when President Barack Obama's nomination of Merrick Garland was, amid much fervent discussion, left to lapse by a Republican-controlled Senate until after the election of President Donald Trump, at which time the seat was filled by a Trump appointee. Even as political constituents reminded Republican senators about their words from 2016, no amount of reminder seemed to shame them into engaging a "straight" way by honoring Justice Ginsburg's final wish and upholding previous precedent. I write about this historic moment as an example of White supremacist authoritarianism being able to stand upright in whatever room it finds itself. Harris-Perry argues that this is not the same for Black women. I quote her definition of shame:

> The emotion of shame has three important elements. The first is social. Individuals feel ashamed in response to a real or imagined audience. We do not feel shame in isolation, only when we transgress a social boundary or break a community expectation. Our internal moral guide may lead us to feel guilt, but shame comes when we fear exposure and evaluation by others. This may be especially true for girls and women, who draw a larger sense of self-identity from their friendly, familial, and romantic relationships. Second, shame is global. It causes us not only to evaluate our actions but to

make a judgment about our whole selves. A person may feel guilty about a specific incident but still feel that she is a good person. Shame is more divisive; it extends beyond a single incident and becomes an evaluation of the self. Psychologists commonly refer to shame as a belief in the malignant self: the idea that your entire person is infected by something inherently bad and potentially contagious. Finally, shame brings a psychological and physical urge to withdraw, submit, or appease others. When we feel ashamed, we tend to *drop our heads*, avert our eyes, and fold into ourselves. . . . Shame makes us want to be smaller, timid, and more closed. Shame transforms our identity. We experience ourselves as being small and worthless and as being exposed.[3]

So, what is the point of understanding microaggression and shame? I argue that microaggression and shaming work especially well against minoritized identities. By "minoritized identities" I mean women, Black and minoritized bodies, Indigenous people, folk of Asian descent, etc. With that being said, scholars argue that as a society we must respond to the harm and shame of microaggressive acts because we have a responsibility to provide healing aid for such cumulative harm. Indeed, associate professor of philosophy Saba Fatima teaches that creating an environment where individual responsibility includes initiatives such as self-education about microaggression, self-reflection about one's implicit biases, and learning about how these biases contribute to one's microaggressive behavior is essential to begin healing.

Now, I am very much aware that some may argue that microaggression and shame are tools of liberal scholars that theoretically and practically do more harm than good. In their book *The Coddling of the American Mind*, Greg Lukianoff and Jonathan Haidt

---

3. Harris-Perry, *Sister Citizen*, 50 (emphasis added).

create pushback by arguing that American universities are culti-
vating fragile psyches in students, encouraging them to protest
anything that makes them slightly uncomfortable.[4] According to
Lukianoff and Haidt, such policing of unintentional slights ensures
that students cannot go on to fulfill the intellectual demands of life
after college. In their chapter "The Untruth of Us versus Them,"
they compare and contrast "common humanity" identity politics
with "common enemy" identity politics. Essentially, they argue
that emphasizing how a White male is at the top of a power hier-
archy is not helpful and that those who do engage identity politics
should do so in the vein of Martin Luther King Jr.: by embracing a
beloved community of common humanity. Other scholars extend
the work of Lukianoff and Haidt in order to argue that a "culture of
victim mentality" follows college students after graduation. Saba
Fatima employs the work of Regina Rini as a way of responding to
such claims. Rini's statement deserves quoting in full:

> The new culture of victimhood is not new, and it is not about
> victimhood. It is a culture of solidarity, and it has always been
> with us, an underground moral culture of the disempowered.
> In the culture of solidarity, individuals who cannot enforce
> their honor or dignity instead make claim on recognition of
> their simple humanity. They publicize mistreatment not be-
> cause they enjoy the status of victim but *because they need the
> support of others to remain strong,* and because public discom-
> fort is the only possible route to redress.[5]

For the purpose of this book, I would argue that hindering
those who call out microaggressions is an attempt to keep those

4. Greg Lukianoff and Jonathan Haidt, *The Coddling of the American
Mind: How Good Intentions and Bad Ideas Are Setting Up a Generation for
Failure* (New York: Penguin, 2018).
5. Quoted in Fatima, "I Know What Happened," 165.

on the underside of society from speaking out against the powers that be. Rini's statement underscores the solidarity of disempowered individuals. Additionally, I would argue that if the oppressed do not support one another and remain strong, public discomfort disappears without pressure. Consider the importance of collectively and publicly remembering George Floyd's death. Microaggressive acts not only discomfort the recipient; they are also part of an overall system of domination that led to Floyd's death over the course of eight minutes and forty-six seconds. Floyd's death was a moment in which the whole world saw what Black and minoritized folks have been seeing for centuries, though we were often told that our eyes deceived us.

"Gaslighting" Defined

Gaslighting occurs when folks around a microaggressed person doubt or question the reality of the microaggressed person and even the microaggressive incident. A specifically Christian example would be that when a woman experiences an unfulfilled call to ministry, the men exercising authoritarianism around her may state that because the inerrant and infallible biblical text says women must experience fulfillment in childbearing or in being obedient to a husband, her real lived sense of unfulfillment is not valid. She must pray her way out of such thoughts and feelings.

In another scenario, a Black woman in a Christian organization may voice dissatisfaction because she experiences racial microaggression, but the authoritarian folks in leadership suggest she is angry and that she needs to pray for a better way to control her anger. Did her supervisors ask, "Why is she angry?" Well, she may be angry that the administration wants her to teach only the "plain sense" of the biblical text without raising any awareness of racial and cultural differences. She is bringing too much of herself and "the voices of her people" to students who only need to hear about

Jesus.[6] In the midst of this conversation, she is then advised to pray for healing of her anger so that she will see that engaging the plain sense of the biblical text is better for students than thinking critically about connections between oppressed people in the text and oppressed people today.

I follow Fatima in defining gaslighting as when "the hearer of testimony (typically about a harm or injustice committed against the speaker) raises doubts about the speaker's reliability at perceiving events accurately."[7] A common response of someone who hears about a microaggressive incident is an attempt to explain to the microaggressed person that what they heard or how they felt is not really what happened. Oftentimes they will try to offer an alternative explanation of the incident—most often without even having been there when it occurred. Repeatedly, interlocutors may offer explanations such as "Surely they did not mean it like that" or "They were just trying to help you." Or, regarding the biblical text, someone may say, "Well, the Bible says, 'Let every person be subject to the governing authorities'" as a way to advise the marginalized person that they do not have any power and must submit to the "governing authorities" of their organization.[8]

The doctrines of biblical inerrancy and infallibility that occur in White supremacist authoritarianism often lead to the epistemic harm of gaslighting and even produce people who become complicit in their own oppression. Folks who experience microaggressions unto gaslighting are made to doubt their reality and even what they see before their eyes or feel within their bodies. Women,

6. If you have not already read Chanequa Walker-Barnes's book *I Bring the Voices of My People* (Grand Rapids: Eerdmans, 2019), add it to your reading list right now.

7. Fatima, "I Know What Happened," 168.

8. This translation of Romans 13:1 is from the New Revised Standard Version.

and specifically African American women, have been taught to doubt what we see even in the biblical text.

Sight! (After the Gaslighting)

In her phenomenal book *I'm Still Here: Black Dignity in a World Made for Whiteness*, Austin Channing Brown describes what having a Black marketing professor meant during her formative college years. She discovers she did not have to decode White middle-class experiences for herself during this particular class. As I read Brown's work, I realized I had to decode while reading Bible studies written by White women. I also realized I was never good at decoding White middle-class ideals.

When I was in my first marriage, I often read books on purity by Elisabeth Elliot or books about the "proper way" to be a Christian wife so that you spend less money on electricity. One of the ways I was told to save money was to let my hair air-dry instead of "wasting" the fifty cents or so blow-drying my hair. This advice works well for a White woman, but for a Black woman who at this time was trying to keep a straight (White woman's) hairstyle, blow-drying was my only option. However, thanks to the heyday of natural hairstyles for African American women, I no longer feel pressured to stick to straight hairstyles as a sign of my deference to Eurocentric beauty standards.

Consider another example. After beginning my first teaching job in Seattle, I was selected to attend a new faculty orientation with the Association of Theological Schools, the accrediting body for theological schools and seminaries in the United States and Canada. At one of our meetings I met another new faculty person, from another institution, who proceeded to tell me that I "took his job." The microaggression behind such a statement is the idea that because I am an African American woman, the search committee pushed my application to the front in order to boast "diversity" in their hiring. The epistemic harm that occurs when folks nonchalantly comment on why African American women get jobs fills the recipient (me) with self-doubt.

Even though for a split second I was filled with self-doubt, I have to admit that I bounced back quickly simply out of necessity and self-preservation. When the gentleman told me I took his job, I replied, "Oh, really? Tell me what you teach." My interlocutor began to regale me with courses that are strictly historical-critical or in the vein of "White male biblical scholar." I proceeded to ask him if he taught Womanist or feminist interpretations of the Bible, to which he responded in the negative. I also asked if, perhaps, he integrated critical social theories into his biblical interpretations. Again, he answered negatively. At that juncture I responded that I teach and engage those modalities, and therefore I did not take his job, since my institution needed those classes, that training, for its students.

For many White Christians who espouse White supremacist authoritarian stances in their biblical interpretations, personal identity while reading, they say, should mean nothing.[9] A statement I heard often in various contexts was "Angela, we don't need you to be our *Black* New Testament professor, we just need you just to be our New Testament professor." In my head, I heard, "We need you to be our White male biblical scholar." What this particular gaslighting position underscores is that most organizations and the folks within said organizations do not want to engage with the intersectionality that my embodied identity encompasses.

Traditional, historical-critical practices within biblical scholarship *must* engage with the real lived experiences of a multiplic-

9. Other scholars, however, are very deliberately engaging personal identity in biblical interpretation, such as Esau McCaulley in *Reading While Black: African American Biblical Interpretation as an Exercise in Hope* (Downers Grove, IL: InterVarsity, 2020).

ity of identities, Womanist identity included.[10] Black women's lived experience and Black women's reasoning must be brought to bear in the reading of the biblical text, providing an avenue for churched African American women to experience power and testimonial authority stemming from biblical authority and not the stifled breathing brought on by White supremacist authoritarianism in the present age of Black Lives Matter.

Finding Power and Voice after the Gaslighting

Again I will move to some work in critical social theory in order to engage my lived experience with what I read in the biblical text. Two books by Patricia Hill Collins are important for understanding power, racism, and intersectionality as interpretive tools for my Womanist engagement.[11] In her earlier work, *Black Feminist Thought*, Collins aids my understanding of Womanist ideas of power and power relations in a number of ways. As she theorizes a politics of empowerment, she questions the dialectical relationship that seemingly does not link oppression and activism. More specifically, she explicitly states that for Black women, thinking through power is not simply an intellectual activity but is representative of real life. What you should begin to see is that Collins helps me connect real life to how inerrancy and infallibility actually work on real bodies. Activism and resistance are inherent to power relations, and both contemporary women and women within the biblical text must find connections of shared activism

10. See Angela Parker, "Reading Mary Magdalene with Stacey Abrams," in *Come and Read: Interpretative Approaches in the Gospel of John*, ed. Alicia D. Myers and Lindsey S. Jodrey (Lanham, MD: Lexington Books/Fortress Academic, 2019).

11. Patricia Hill Collins, *Black Feminist Thought: Knowledge, Consciousness, and the Politics of Empowerment* (New York: Routledge, 2000); and *Intersectionality as Critical Social Theory* (Durham, NC: Duke University Press, 2019).

and resistance. Such a reading of texts, because it engages cultural issues, is counter to the readings that the doctrines of inerrancy and infallibility allow. Where do women have a modicum of power that we may exert in our reading of the biblical text? Further, since power is not something a group possesses but is, in fact, an intangible entity that operates within a matrix of domination wherein people stand in varying relationships, Collins prompts me to ask what women's engagement with community looks like, as women are gendered participants in the early Jesus community.[12]

In *Intersectionality as Critical Social Theory*, Collins moves to a model that is important for my understanding of expanding biblical interpretation. Intersectionality is a concept that highlights the metaphorical and paradigmatic ways in which race, class, gender, and sexuality are all modes of identity that have ramifications in oppressive social, political, and academic places of domination. Collins states that "intersectionality must consider how the demographics of intersectional communities and the epistemic standards that characterize those communities influence its own critical inquiry."[13] Put in faith terms, is there a way that faith communities can think about their own diversities without overpowering those in marginalized positions?

As I tell students, the concept of intersectionality is designed to help members of a community see their blind spots. If some communities, specifically evangelical communities that espouse inerrancy and infallibility, do not engage ways of interrogating their own blind spots, how can they imagine full and complete readings of the biblical text? In my Womanist New Testament mind, watching how some interpretative communities (namely, White male biblical scholars) read women in the text without recognizing women's intersectionality is highly problematic. Epistemic priv-

12. Collins, *Black Feminist Thought*, 274.
13. Collins, *Intersectionality*, 128.

ilege and power become important details to wrestle with when scholars engage academic thought and activist praxis. Primarily, Collins's work serves as a basis for an interpretative stance that asks how testimonial authority is a form of epistemic resistance that challenges the taken-for-granted thinking of White male biblical scholars who hold a White supremacist authoritarian view of the biblical text.

All my argumentation is leading toward the idea that "color blindness" or assimilation is the goal of White supremacist authoritarianism that stems from the doctrines of inerrancy and infallibility. Diversity and inclusion in many congregations simply means "add some Black folk and stir." I would argue that any biblical reading that does not pay attention to the ways in which women and racialized people in the biblical text engage oppression is not likely to engage the fullness and complexity of the text. Just as Black and minoritized folks suffer marginalization in many ecclesial settings, there are bodies within the New Testament text that suffer similar marginalization as a result of living in a Roman imperial system. To reclaim my Womanist identity after moments of gaslighting, I often have to take "Sankofa" moments and "go back" psychologically into the past to read beyond assimilation and color blindness.

Sankofa is a philosophical tradition and system originating in Ghana and developed further through Black American culture during and after enslavement.[14] Translating to "it is not wrong to go back for that which you have forgotten," Sankofa offers a solution to reconstituting a fragmented cultural past and identity that may have been lost.[15] It is the process of expanding ways of understanding and critiquing experiences through a racial and

14. Pamela Felder Small, Marco J. Barker, and Marybeth Gasman, eds., *Sankofa: African American Perspectives on Race and Culture in US Doctoral Education* (Albany: State University of New York Press, 2020).
15. See editors' introduction in *Sankofa*, 1–17.

cultural lens for Black folks. For me, as a Womanist New Testament scholar, Sankofa also represents resistance and rejection of Eurocentric language and worldviews while insisting on the relevance of using African concepts to define and characterize African life in the contemporary era. I would argue that there is a Sankofa moment, a "returning to the source" to reclaim lost identity, in the Gospel of Mark that speaks to women and sight in the midst of gaslighting.

Sight after Gaslighting in the Gospel of Mark

At the end of the Gospel of Mark there is a curious aside that should make every reader and hearer of Mark say, "Wait, what?" In Mark 15:40–41, the writer casually states that there were women who had been following Jesus from the beginning of his ministry in Galilee. However, from the entire fifteen chapters prior, one would not get even an inkling of an idea that women were serving as disciples (that is, following Jesus). Indeed, particular inerrant and infallible readings of the biblical text maintain the illusion of patriarchal power, which projects the idea that only men were chosen to be disciples of Jesus. The aside in Mark 15 is a perfect opportunity for a Sankofa moment in the biblical text. Were it not for African American thought, many of us would not even think to probe this mention of women because we have been trained to think in a White cultural worldview. What happens when the female Holy Spirit whispers, "Go back and get those women"?

Scholars of the Gospel of Mark believe Mark was the first Gospel written, probably between 66 and 70 CE, during the Jewish War against Rome. The context of war is important for proper interpretation of the Gospel, since scholars know the Jewish nation stopped paying taxes to the Roman Empire as a show of revolt. Nonetheless, Rome exerted ultimate power by breaching the walls of Jerusalem and destroying a pivotal part of Jewish identity: the temple. The war against Rome was especially egregious because women's proximity to militaristic forces put women in precarious positions. For example, the Jewish writer Josephus relays the horrific story of the Jewish woman who boils her baby to serve rebel troops because all the food had run out. War is not kind to women, infants, and children.[16]

The Gospel of Mark functions as a two-level drama, talking about Jesus's crucifixion from years prior while the Jewish War was going on in the Gospel writer's present. Because the Gospel writer does not mention women following Jesus from Galilee until 15:40, I ask my seminary students: Knowing that women were always there, how do we reread some of Jesus's conversations with his disciples from Mark 1 to Mark 15? The sudden emergence of women at the crucifixion of Jesus would have definitely jolted the original auditors'[17] attention.

Scholars debate whether these women were "proper disciples."[18] Even as some argue that the women were an afterthought in the Gospel narrative, I tend to disagree. As readers, we cannot understand the intentions of the biblical writers because we cannot ask them face-to-face. And here lies part of the problem behind inerrancy and infallibility. If God is the author, and we also

16. You should hear "WIC" in this sentence. WIC is shorthand for the Special Supplemental Nutrition Program for Women, Infants, and Children, which provides federal grants to states for supplemental foods, healthcare referrals, and nutrition education for low-income, pregnant, and postpartum women, and to infants and children up to age five who are found to be at nutritional risk. I know many women (Black, White, Hispanic, etc.) who benefit from WIC and do not want to see such a program depleted because certain groups think of these as entitlements, even as big corporations get entitlements from government bailouts. See https://www.fns.usda.gov/wic.

17. I believe, and a majority of scholars concur, that the Gospel was first told in an oral tradition.

18. See Raymond E. Brown, *Death of the Messiah: From Gethsemane to the Grave; A Commentary on the Passion Narratives in the Four Gospels* (New York: Doubleday, 1994), 1156.

have the Gospel writer as the author and who is writing in a particular cultural context, then whose intentionality are we pondering? Even if the "intent" of the Gospel writer was not to consider the women "proper disciples," I contend that the original female auditors of the Markan narrative would have heard it in a different way and perhaps similarly to how women today "hear" the crucifixion narrative differently from men.[19]

"Gazing" in Mark 15:40-47

[40]There were also women gazing (theōreō) from a distance. Among them was Mary of Magdala, Mary the mother of Jacob the less and of Josias, and Salome.

19. A significant number of feminist Markan scholars have interrogated the appearance of the women at this juncture of the Markan narrative. While noting that the narrative gives Jesus's women disciples very little visibility and even less voice, Joan L. Mitchell argues that it gives readers permission to see women disciples with Jesus throughout his ministry from its beginning in Galilee to its end in Jerusalem at the cross, burial, and empty tomb; see *Beyond Fear and Silence: A Feminist-Literary Reading of Mark* (New York: Continuum, 2001), 8-9. Elisabeth Schüssler Fiorenza acknowledges the women as "true disciples" in *In Memory of Her: A Feminist Theological Reconstruction of Christian Origins*, 10th anniv. ed. (New York: Herder & Herder, 1994), 320. Following Elizabeth Struthers Malbon (who argues that the male disciples proved fallible), and Winsome Munro, Susan Miller argues that the women act as foils to the twelve male disciples; see *Women in Mark's Gospel* (New York: T&T Clark International, 2004), 153-73. Hisako Kinukawa, in her book *Women and Jesus in Mark: A Japanese Feminist Perspective* (Maryknoll, NY: Orbis, 1994), 90-106, argues that the women serve as role models of "life-giving" suffering and were examples of challenge to the male disciples, who avoided the struggles of the oppressed. Korean feminist postcolonial scholar Seong Hee Kim offers a "Salim" ("making things alive") interpretation of these women as present in an apocalyptic cross of life wherein they are precursors to Korean women who fulfill a model of discipleship in a situation of suffering; see *Mark, Women and Empire: A Korean Postcolonial Perspective* (Sheffield: Sheffield Phoenix Press, 2010), 117-32.

⁴¹When in Galilee, these [women] were following him and ministering to him, and many others [women] were going up with him to Jerusalem.

⁴²And after evening was coming, it was the preparation which is the Sabbath.

⁴³Joseph, the one from Arimathea, a prominent council member (who also himself was anticipating the kingdom of God), boldly went unto Pilate and requested the body of Jesus.

⁴⁴But Pilate marveled if already he had died and called a centurion and asked him if he had died so soon.

⁴⁵And knowing from the centurion, he granted the corpse to Joseph.

⁴⁶And after buying a fine linen cloth and taking him down, he wrapped him in the fine linen cloth and placed him in a tomb, which was hewn from rock, and placed a stone in the door of the tomb.

⁴⁷And Mary of Magdala and Mary the mother of Josias were gazing (*theōreō*) upon where he was placed.[20]

There are two Greek words for "to see" in the Gospel of Mark. The first is *blepō*, which is just a basic seeing, a perceiving; this is the word the Gospel writer uses most frequently prior to chapter 15.[21] The second word is *theōreō*, and it implies deep contemplation, consideration, observation, and inspection. In Mark 15:40–47, *theōreō* frames the passage, appearing in verses 40 and 47. When I think about this passage, I'm struck by how the women are described as "gazing" as opposed to simply seeing.

It seems to me that the Gospel of Mark begs for a hermeneutic that interrogates the idea of gazing. Foucault's language of the

20. This is my own translation.
21. See Mark 4:12, 24; 5:31; 8:15, 18, 23–24; 12:14, 38; 13:2, 5, 9, 23, 33.

gaze emphasizes the fact that even when there is a network of gazes, part of the power behind the gaze is how the gaze is deployed. Thinking back to microaggression and shaming, I would argue that the power of microaggression and shame stems from the idea that those with greater "seeing" or "gazing" power can inflict hurt and shame on oppressed people. As I read the Gospel of Mark, I have to ask how the women actually claim a moment of assertiveness and resistance even in their simple act of gazing. Therefore, I argue that these women are not simply "looking" at some circumstance; they are actively gazing upon a situation in order to ponder their next action.

After thinking about their gaze, I wonder what the women's upright positionality would be. Can they "stand straight in a crooked room"? If not, who has the power and privilege to do so? The Gospel writer tells us that Joseph of Arimathea requests the body of Jesus. When one considers the fact that these women are intensely contemplating what they are gazing upon, it seems apropos to imagine that they are looking at a privileged man—who did not walk with them as a disciple of Jesus—request Jesus's body for burial.

In essence, I argue the plausibility of women experiencing feelings around extreme lack of privilege. The women are not allowed to get close to the scene to handle their deceased loved one and leader. They appear to lack relationship with Joseph of Arimathea. If the women were in Jesus's close company, and if Joseph *was* a disciple, as some scholars argue, why did the women and Joseph not converse about burying Jesus?[22] Scholars who do read and in-

---

22. Others who engage this text include Miller, *Women in Mark's Gospel*, 153–73; Kinukawa, *Women and Jesus in Mark*, 90–106; and Kim, *Mark, Women and Empire*, 117–32; all treat the women in Mark 15:40–47 separately from Joseph of Arimathea. Other scholars who read the women separately from Joseph of Arimathea include Morna D. Hooker, *The Gospel according to Mark* (London: A & C Black, 1991), 374–82; Robert H. Gundry, *Mark: A Com-

terpret some kind of relationship between Joseph and the women tend to interpret the women in a negative light for not assisting Joseph even if their own proximity to soldiers would place them in bodily harm. Scholars focus positively on Joseph, however, without attention to the nuance of gender.[23] Even in commentaries the women tend to receive negative interpretations. Gaslighting and microaggression occur even in scholarly work on this passage.

Concluding Thoughts on Gaslighting

So what does this small foray into gaslighting and women in the biblical text demonstrate? I would argue that if someone holds a view of inerrancy and infallibility from a White supremacist authoritarian orientation, the biblical women suffer gaslighting twice: first by the men in the text, and then by the scholars who proclaim the women to be "improper" disciples. Moreover, contemporary readers of the biblical text suffer gaslighting interpretations, since we are trained through the doctrines of inerrancy and infallibility not to question the text and not to question the White

---

mentary on His Apology for the Cross (Grand Rapids: Eerdmans, 1993), 979–88; Douglas R. A. Hare, *Mark* (Louisville: Westminster John Knox, 1996), 219; Richard A. Horsley, *Hearing the Whole Story: The Politics of Plot in Mark's Gospel* (Louisville: Westminster John Knox, 2001), 205; Theodore W. Jennings Jr., *The Insurrection of the Crucified: The "Gospel of Mark" as Theological Manifesto* (Chicago: Exploration Press, 2003), 297–301; and Joel Marcus, *Mark 8–16: A New Translation with Introduction and Commentary* (New Haven: Yale University Press, 2009), 1053–78.

23. One of the scholars who reads the women and Joseph of Arimathea together textually (without any personal relationship) is Ched Myers in *Binding the Strong Man: A Political Reading of Mark's Story of Jesus* (Maryknoll, NY: Orbis, 1994), 392–97. Myers actually reads the centurion, Joseph, and the women as "Aftermath: Responses to Jesus's Death." Laurel K. Cobb also reads the women with Joseph of Arimathea; see *Mark and Empire: Feminist Reflections* (Maryknoll, NY: Orbis, 2013), 165–66.

male interpreter who expounds the text from a White supremacist authoritarian viewpoint.

Questions for Consideration

Perhaps "microaggression" and "gaslighting" are new to your vocabulary. Take a moment to ponder where you have been a micro-aggressed person or a microaggressor. After reading this chapter, what have you learned about yourself or about previous actions and incidents? As a child growing up in Black Baptist churches, I would often hear, "When you know better, you do better." That is my prayer for all of us.

Chapter 4

MOVING FROM STIFLED BREATH
TO FULL-THROATED FAITH

Having expounded on gaslighting in biblical interpretation, I now turn to ponder mature faith formation by reconceptualizing the doctrinal idea of "faith in Jesus Christ" as "walking in the faith of Jesus Christ" unto death—that is, social death to White supremacist authoritarianism in faith communities. My foray into this conversation begins with my love of reading and translating the Greek text of the New Testament, which enables a nuanced reading of Galatians 1:1 and 2:16. Moreover, my engagement of translation, exegesis, and the history of interpretation serves my argument that part of the Galatians text's final exhortation is that all of us simply "make it home."

Two issues propel me to engage the ideas of "walking in the faith of Jesus" and "making it home." Recently, my colleague Chanequa Walker-Barnes preached in our chapel and played a haunting video prior to her preaching moment. The video was a rap song titled "Make It Home" by Tobe Nwigwe. Dear reader, I implore you at this moment to play the YouTube video of Nwigwe's song so that you have context for my Womanist reading of Paul's letter to the church at Galatia. As I have taught this letter, I have often put forth the idea that the work of the Galatian community was to walk each other home. Similarly, contemporary Jesus followers are charged with ensuring that we all "make it home"—"bearing one another's burdens" (Gal. 6:2), and so on. In this chapter I will argue that moving from stifled breath to full-throated faith demands a reimagination of faith in the Galatian text.

Some of the questions I bring to this chapter include the following. How are we to read and teach Paul from within the context of the United States when various citizens and bodies are still constantly devalued even in faith communities? How are we to understand the highly creedal language of "faith" in Galatians 2:16 as it relates to the issues of inerrancy and infallibility? What is salvation, and does it have any connection to actual bodies in the Galatian text and in our contemporary context? Or does "salvation" refer only to a Lutheran idea of justification by faith in Jesus Christ? What ought we to make of the church's privileging "faith in Christ" as the most important element for our understanding of Christian identity? How is the phrase "faith in Christ" related to the doctrines of inerrancy and infallibility? To begin, I will unpack why translation work is important for combatting White supremacist authoritarianism.

Why Translating from Biblical Greek Is Important (to Me)

One thing I have been doing at the start of each semester is asking students what their nonnegotiables are for classroom management. Now, not every nonnegotiable will become a part of the classroom learning covenant, but I do like to open up the conversation for students to think about how they are part of their learning journey. During this time, I put forth my own: "You cannot begin a sentence with, 'The Bible says . . .'" Often, students are stunned. Many of us have grown up saying, "The Bible says . . ." as a way to halt a conversation or win an argument. However, during the course of a semester I train my students, when citing the Bible, to quote both book and verse rather than using the generic attribution "the Bible." Students then begin to realize the nuances of quoting from the Gospel of John versus the writings of Paul, for example, and how the underlying contexts (both cultural and linguistic) of each may be different and not simply harmonized together. There is a reason I invoke this nonnegotiable, and it stems from the Greek language.

One of the great pleasures of my professional life is teaching Greek to seminary students. Taking the time to learn the morphology, syntax, and grammar of a language is slow and hard but so rewarding for students. As students begin to learn Greek, they begin to understand that the biblical text is not easily translatable into English in a one-to-one correspondence. There are nuances in translation. Moreover, I advise students that early doctrines of inspiration have been restricted to the manuscripts in Hebrew, Greek, or Aramaic. Early doctrines did not hold translations to be inspired. As students begin to understand that language learning yields interpretative options, they have to make a decision on how to adjudicate those options. Again, the multitude of decisions forces students to slow down and, dare I say, become less hermeneutically arrogant. As a professor, the loss of hermeneutical arrogance is truly a blessing to my life!

I often tell students I have not had the luxury of living in certainty. Yes, I live and walk in and by faith, but faith is not certainty. Let me say that one more time: FAITH IS NOT CERTAINTY. Paul's letter to the Galatians is an excellent text with which to think through my own faith walk. There are many translations of Galatians 2:16, for example, that diminish what certainty looks like. So the first question for me becomes: What translation theories do I submit to as a Womanist New Testament scholar who dwells in the land of uncertainty yet dwells there by faith?

First, I would say that I attempt a certain "faithfulness" to Womanist thinking as I engage translation theory. One of my best White feminist scholar mentors, Tina Pippin, argues that part of translation work is to answer questions pertaining to the silence of popular and legitimized academic translations on issues of gender, race and class.[1] Pippin recognizes that in the history of Bible translation there is a sense of being "faithful" that often can bring in oppressive material. So then the question becomes: Should the translator be faithful to the text even if that means bringing oppressive material to the faith community? How can one begin to provide a "faithful" translation of the biblical text while also being faithful to the political, social, and cultural positionalities that one may be a part of? How can one provide a "faithful" translation without bringing harm to a community?

I truly believe that biblical scholars who are aware of the cultural elements of translation must pay specific attention to the effects on embodied identities. Scholars must understand that traditional translation theory can oftentimes affect real human lives in disastrous ways. As one way out of the conundrum, I agree with Pippin that translators must recognize the ethical issues at the heart of all translations and not seek simply to smooth everything out for easy or palatable understandings. While the powers that be may use protective strategies to contain various ways that the biblical text can "mean" within faith communities, part of my call as a Womanist New Testament scholar is to embrace the cultural boundedness of the biblical text and of the people I preach to and teach. In this way I follow scholars like Pippin, who advocates for "activist translation" in which I can identify "transformational translation or translation for social change."[2]

Now, I have to confess that I am not the only African American scholar to show how translation actually upholds White supremacist authoritarianism. Clarice P. Martin began this process for many

1. Tina Pippin, "Translation Happens: A Feminist Perspective on Translation Theories," in *Escaping Eden: New Feminist Perspectives on the Bible*, ed. Harold C. Washington, Susan Lochrie Graham, and Pamela Thimmes (New York: New York University Press, 1999), 163–76.
2. Pippin, "Translation Happens," 169.

Womanists.[3] Martin's work questions the proper translation of the Greek word *doulos* in Pauline literature. In some translations the word is "servant," which evokes images of British servants bringing tea to upper-class families, while in other translations the word is rendered "slave," which gives a different connotation entirely. Martin argues convincingly that translations that decontextualize Roman imperial slavery actually uphold and support White ideals.

Other African American biblical scholars who engage translation theory include Randall Bailey and Wil Gafney. Bailey deconstructs Whiteness in Isaiah, cogently arguing that the formula "to be made white as snow" in Isaiah 1:18 is not a blessing in the Hebrew Bible but is, in fact, a curse. White supremacist societies have used the history of interpretation for this passage to argue Whiteness as a sign of purity and thus as a desirable outcome for which one should strive.[4] Bailey deconstructs the formula by addressing three vital areas. First, he addresses the issue of the translation history of Isaiah 1:18 by showing how much of White supremacist interpretations of biblical passages, which buttressed the slave trade and subsequent dehumanization of African peoples, can be traced back to early rabbinic teachings in the midrashim and Talmud. Citing Charles Copher, Bailey addresses the continued belief that "turning black" was the curse of both Cain in Genesis 4 and Ham in the story of Noah.[5] Even though there is no mention of

3. Clarice J. Martin, "The Haustafeln (Household Codes) in African American Biblical Interpretation: 'Free Slaves' and 'Subordinate Women,'" in *Stony the Road We Trod: African American Biblical Interpretation*, ed. Cain Hope Felder (Minneapolis: Fortress, 1991), 206–31; Clarice J. Martin, "Womanist Interpretations of the New Testament: The Quest for Holistic and Inclusive Translation and Interpretation," *Journal of Feminist Studies in Religion* 6, no. 2 (Fall 1990): 41–61.

4. Randall C. Bailey, "We Shall Become White as Snow: When Bad Is Turned into Good," *Semeia* 76 (December 1998): 99.

5. Bailey, "We Shall Become White as Snow," 101.

color in either of these stories, these arguments began in rabbinic literature and were perpetuated throughout the Enlightenment. They continued in the sanctioned reasoning behind the African slave trade and allowed European countries to continue colonization in Africa with no sense of shame whatsoever. Bailey concludes by stating that ideologies of race have played a crucial part in biblical scholarship and that one should not be surprised that they have functioned on the level of translation, since translation is another form of interpretation.[6]

Second, Bailey proceeds to outline, deconstruct, and reevaluate the Eurocentric value of being "white as snow." Highlighting the proliferation of hymns that encourage parishioners to pray for the deity to "make them white as snow," Bailey notes the liturgical calendar's use of lighter colors during seasons of celebration, whereas darker colors are used during seasons of penitence. Bailey does acknowledge that the Roman Catholic Church has turned from black robes to white robes during funerals. This move, however, was done not to deconstruct the negative association of Blackness but to switch to an emphasis on resurrection. These examples show the fixed association, in Western thought, of White with purity and Black with "otherness." Delving into the presumptive value of Whiteness, Bailey concludes that "white as snow" is a sign of curse or disease that has been transformed into a sign of purity in continued contemporary readings and interpretations of Scripture.[7] I would argue that these readings continue to inform what "inerrancy" and "infallibility" actually do to embodied identities in our various faith communities.

Wil Gafney has also influenced my understanding of the importance of translation as a Womanist New Testament scholar.[8]

6. Bailey, "We Shall Become White as Snow," 101.
7. Bailey, "We Shall Become White as Snow," 108-9.
8. See Wilda C. Gafney, *Womanist Midrash: A Reintroduction to the Women of the Torah and the Throne* (Louisville: Presbyterian Publishing,

Because translation is viewed as an invisible act, readers often think it is value- and culture-free, but, as both Pippin and Gafney argue, that is far from the case.

Further, Gafney emphasizes that she has been shaped by the Western scholarly academy. In the ways it shapes and trains scholars, the academy differentiates translation from interpretation, thereby implying that translation is a neutral practice. Gafney argues that the Western scholarly academy has thought of translation as a word-for-word process comparable to a mathematical equation. I find that in my own work and scholarship, both translation and interpretation are predicated upon the idea of objectivity. As I unpacked in chapter 1, objectivity is linked to the exhortation to be a White male biblical scholar. Those who train others in recognizing White supremacy culture show that objectivity and neutrality validate particular people for leadership roles in predominantly White organizations.[9] Hence, Gafney's words are highly important.

> Bible translators have been overwhelmingly White, as is our guild. This means that until very recently, the Bibles that hold authority in my religious and academic worlds were produced by scholars who do not look like me, do not share my culture, and are part of a culture that has been openly hostile to the scholastic capacity, literary achievements, and even moral agency of my people.[10]

2017); and Wil Gafney, "Translation Matters: A Fem/Womanist Exploration of Translation Theory and Practice for Proclamation in Worship," in *Text and Community: Essays in Memory of Bruce M. Metzger* (Sheffield: Sheffield Phoenix, 2007), 55–66.

9. See Tema Okun, "White Supremacy Culture," *Dismantling Racism*, www.dismantlingracism.org/white-supremacy-culture.html.

10. Gafney, *Womanist Midrash*, 247.

Again, authority is connected to a text that is White supremacist in its orientation.

Engaging the White Male Scholar Who Reads Galatians

While I do not embrace every aspect of my training, I must stress that I have learned so much about the apostle Paul's letters as a result of my formative years at Duke Divinity School. Studying with Douglas Campbell and Richard Hays has formed me in ways that in some aspects I run from but in others, embrace.

As I synthesize my own sensibilities in Womanist translation with my training by talented White male biblical scholars in Pauline literature, I recognize two areas that are important for my own scholarship and social activism. First, I will always center the experiences of embodied Black folk as I translate and interpret biblical texts, since, as I have shown, White supremacist authoritarianism remains a constant force in past and continuing interpretations of the biblical text. Second, even as I argue throughout this book that White supremacist authoritarianism must be dismantled, that does not mean I dismantle and demonize all White men. Hear me well! I hope to be a person who can lead and do the things I care about doing in a way that will compel others, including White men, to join me.[11]

My particular Womanist translation sensibility is an interpretative method that takes seriously cultural issues, pushing back against one-sided understandings of certainty in Paul's letter to the Galatians. This method allows nuance and expansion on traditional interpretations of Paul's language in the Galatians text, as I begin at Galatians 1:1, connect that to 2:15, and finish with 6:18. Moving through Galatians from stifled breath to full-throated faith entails the expansion of superficial creedal faith into mature

11. This sentence is a slight paraphrase of a Ruth Bader Ginsburg quote.

faith. My reading of Galatians challenges strictly White supremacist doctrinal ideas of faith, providing instead a Womanist understanding of the term.

The Galatian Context

Before I move to my exegesis of Galatians 2:16, I must first unpack
my understanding of the Galatian context. Scholars have debated
the context of Galatians for years.[12] For the purposes of our conversation, I function under the assumption that Paul's "setting in
life" entails heated argumentation concerning circumcision as a
(Jewish) identity marker for recent converts to the Jesus movement. However, conventional analyses of this context have centered on conversion in relationship to justification and ethics from
a Eurocentric and doctrinal viewpoint.

Put more clearly, I believe one way inerrancy and infallibility have
functioned in our reading of the Galatians text is through an understanding of faith in Jesus Christ that is creedal and separate from an

12. Scholars engaged in this debate include early Galatian scholars who
influenced Martin Luther's understanding of "justification by faith" as an
expression of Christianity versus Judaism. For contextualization, see F. F.
Bruce, *The Epistle to the Galatians: A Commentary on the Greek Text* (Grand
Rapids: Eerdmans, 1982), 1–2. Other scholars have interpreted Galatians
through a lens of the New Perspective on Paul, understanding that Paul
did not take issue with works righteousness and did not believe Judaism
was legalistic. See E. P. Sanders's seminal work, *Paul and Palestinian Judaism* (Minneapolis: Fortress, 1977). Still other scholars engage Paul from an
empire-critical and gender-critical perspective (in other words, Paul was
called to political and social consciousness). In this view, Paul presents a
Jewish-messianic monotheism that subverts and reconfigures the claims
of imperial monotheism put forth by the Roman Empire. See Brigitte Kahl,
Galatians Re-Imagined: Reading with the Eyes of the Vanquished, Paul in Critical Contexts (Minneapolis: Fortress, 2010); and Davina Lopez, *Apostle to
the Conquered: Reimagining Paul's Mission*, Paul in Critical Contexts (Minneapolis: Fortress, 2009).

idea of "walking by the faith of Jesus the Christ" as we walk with one another to "make it home." Accordingly, I do not believe scholars have paid enough attention to the Roman imperial context as it relates to Judaism, Galatian identity, and the Galatians' relationship to faith that is not predicated on an internal understanding of faith in Jesus as the only option. I will discuss the Roman imperial context further after my discussion on the narrative structure of Galatians.

White Male Biblical Scholar Richard Hays and the Jesus Narrative in Galatians

As I have already pointed out, I was blessed and fortunate to study with both Richard Hays and Douglas Campbell, two esteemed scholars of Pauline literature. Not surprisingly, Hays's *The Faith of Jesus Christ* took the Pauline scholarly world by storm.[13] In this book Hays makes two claims about Galatians that are relevant for my work. First, the framework of Paul's thought is not a system of doctrines but the story of Jesus, which the early Jesus followers at Galatia were caught up into, acting it out in the narrative of their own lives. Second, Hays argues that Paul lays out the gospel through his own christological understanding of a "participatory" salvation history. Hays reads Galatians 3:1, 13-14, 22, 26-28, and 4:3-6 as representative of Paul's understanding of the Jesus story. The way the Jesus follower "participates" in that story comes to full expression, Hays says, in the language of *pistis Iēsou Christou* in 3:22 (and twice in 2:16). I follow Hays's insistence that *pistis Iēsou Christou* should be taken as a subjective genitive as opposed to an objective genitive.

There has been much ink spilled to explain the difference between the subjective and objective genitive readings of *pistis*

13. Richard B. Hays, *The Faith of Jesus Christ: The Narrative Substructure of Galatians 3:1–4:11*, 2nd ed. (Grand Rapids: Eerdmans, 2002).

Iēsou Christou in Galatians. Essentially it comes down to the idea that Paul thinks either that a believer has faith in Jesus (objective genitive) or that Jesus had faith that God would raise him from the dead (subjective genitive). In the context of the *pistis Iēsou Christou* debate, many pastors, preachers, and teachers argue that a believer's faith in Christ is of utmost importance for salvation.

While it is interesting to think about faith in Pauline literature, I must note that Paul never actually defines faith. Scholars like Rudolf Bultmann conclude that the phrase *pistis Iēsou Christou* means Jesus died and rose from the dead according to Paul's earliest writing in 1 Thessalonians 5:14.[14] Faith, by nature, is always directed "into" something, Bultmann says. For Bultmann, the only logical idea of faith is personal faith that unites one to Christ and then unites all such individuals as a covenant community "in Christ." Jesus is the object of faith. That's objective genitive.

The *subjective* genitive, on the other hand, focuses not on the faith that the Christian has in Jesus's sacrifice but on Jesus's own faithfulness to walk in the way of sacrifice, knowing he may not "make it home." This differentiation will be part of my translation of Galatians 2:16.

The beauty of Hays's work is that he does not argue that there is only one right understanding of *pistis Iēsou Christou* in the Galatians text. Can you imagine who does? Yes, more traditional, evangelical White male scholars who hold to inerrant and infallible views of the biblical text. The question then becomes, can we live in a world where we hold both ideas in tension? Most scholars respond negatively to this question, insisting that the tension would cause everything to fall apart. You can imagine, dear reader, that I answer in the affirmative.

---

14. G. Kittel, G. W. Bromiley, and G. Friedrich, eds., *Theological Dictionary of the New Testament*, vol. 6 (Grand Rapids: Eerdmans, 1969), 203.

Some critiques of Hays's work include the fact that even as he acknowledges that *pistis* is not a univocal concept for Paul and is sometimes used ambiguously in Pauline literature, he fails to make more allowance for Paul to speak about believers' faith in different contexts. Specifically, is *pistis* the same in the context of Corinth as it is in the context of Galatia? Instead he tries to make Paul entirely consistent. This is another issue with inerrancy and infallibility. When White supremacist authoritarianism reads biblical texts, all the texts must read similarly. However, Paul is not consistent because he writes to various churches in diverse contexts. It is imperative for contemporary readers of Scripture to understand that concept so that we do not fall into the traps of continued White supremacist authoritarianism that allow no cultural diversity whatsoever as we read the biblical text.

The Dying Gaul. Ancient Roman copy in marble of a now-lost third-century BCE Greek bronze. Capitoline Museum, Rome, Italy.

Dying Galatians; or, Where Do I Place Myself in the Narrative?

One way to broaden the context of Galatians is to pay attention to the Roman imperial context as identified in the work of empire-critical scholars such as Brigitte Kahl and Davina Lopez. These scholars are at the forefront of engaging visual imagery in order to think about the cultural contexts in which Paul was writing to the Galatian church. What is interesting for me is that visual imagery provides another avenue through which I can enter the narrative as an "other" believer, an identity similar to that of the Galatians.

The ancient Greek and Roman elites who had the ability to commission sculptures and other images to highlight victory in battle used the imagery well. Visual imagery served as propaganda to the point that people knew and understood their place. In relationship to the Galatians text, there are two specific images that scholars engage: *The Dying Gaul* and *The Suicidal Gaul*.[15]

Attalus I of the Hellenistic Attalid dynasty commissioned *The Dying Gaul* after his defeat of Galatia in 230 BCE. He erected the bronze statue at the acropolis of Pergamon, the royal capital, as a constant reminder to the Galatians (Celtic Gauls[16]) that the gods had ordained Galatia's submission. The original statue is now lost

---

15. For excellent explanations of both pieces, see C. Gates, *Ancient Cities: The Archaeology of Urban Life in the Ancient Near East and Egypt, Greece, and Rome* (London: Routledge, 2003); and N. Spivey, *Greek Art* (London: Phaidon, 1997).

16. It is always a wonderful teaching moment to talk about the Celtic Gauls to students who have taken classes on Celtic spirituality. Part of the pleasure of teaching is to watch students engage with some of the tenets of Celtic spirituality (such as greater leadership roles for women, love of nature, and an increased call for hospitality) while thinking about how some of these tenets may have evolved from a Galatian community that is part of the Pauline literature.

but is known to us by a surviving marble copy by a Roman artist, which was probably placed in the Gardens of Sallust on the Quirinal Hill to celebrate Julius Caesar's 52 BCE victory over Gaul. In these contexts the statue would have likely communicated the idea that the only good Gaul is a dying Gaul. When I present this image in church settings, I often tell people to substitute "Gaul" with . . . fill in the blank. Immediately church folk can hear "the only good Indian is a dead Indian" or "the only good N-word is a dead N-word." See my point? So how does such contextual information open up an understanding of "faith" that is different from a view of justification by faith alone?

Gaul Killing Himself and His Wife, sometimes known as *The Suicidal Gaul*. Ancient Roman copy in marble of a now-lost third-century BCE Greek bronze. Roman National Museum, Palazzo Altemps, Rome, Italy.

The Suicidal Gaul, also called the *Ludovisi Gaul* after the Roman villa on whose grounds it was later discovered, is another Attalus commission, likely from the same monument. The traditional understanding is that it portrays a married Galatian couple on the losing side of a war; rather than be captured, the man has killed his wife and now plunges a sword into his own chest. The issue I deliberate as I engage *The Suicidal Gaul* is what it means that the Galatian kills his wife instead of allowing them both to fall prey to the Attalids and to submit to enslavement and violation. Since death was better than slavery or continued assault and abuse by rape (for men and women), how can we interpret the limp form of the deceased woman? I have to ask: Did she beg her husband to kill her, or was she taken off guard by her own murder?

Knowing that both *The Dying Gaul* and *The Suicidal Gaul* were ubiquitous in the time of Paul, I will engage some of the scholars who interrogate enslavement and violation of women during the Roman imperial period. Additionally, I will interrogate what the image of the "killed by her husband" Galatian woman may have endured had she been seized as plunder of war.

Destined to Slavery and Repeated Rape?

In other venues I have argued that Paul's self-identification as an enslaved person and as a birthing mother are problematic for embodied identities that embrace both statuses.[17] As other scholars have argued, Paul's religious identity as an apostle of Jesus means he must "birth" the Galatians so that Christ may be shaped in them. Feminist scholars Caroline Osiek and Beverly Roberts Gaventa note that Paul likens himself to a mother to the Gala-

---

17. Angela N. Parker, "One Womanist's View of Racial Reconciliation in Galatians," *Journal of Feminist Studies in Religion* 34, no. 2 (October 2018): 23–40.

tians with the understanding that he is not as far removed from women's experiences as some commentators believe.[18] Osiek argues her point in part by noting that Paul does not discuss apocalyptic time or speak about Hellenistic rebirth. The lack of these factors means, for Osiek, that Paul intended for this metaphor to apply to his ministry alone and was an attempt to solidify closeness to women's bodily experiences. Gaventa, on the other hand, links Paul's language to apocalyptic ideas, understanding Paul's role more broadly as a nurturer of communities. As I have argued elsewhere,[19] I disagree with Osiek and Gaventa for two reasons. First, on the basis of Roman imperial ideas concerning inheritance and adoption (both themes with which Paul wrestles in Galatians), slaves or barbarians must offer up their children to the empire after being enslaved or impregnated.

Additionally, in his allegorization of the Sarah and Hagar story (Gal. 4:21–31), Paul casts the heavenly city, as understood through the matriarch Sarah, as the eternal place of transformation. Paul's midrash rejects Hagar, a slave, and perpetually places her in a subservient position. While Paul's original auditors may have understood the allegorical nature of his argument, what would the allegory have meant for a woman who saw representations of dead Galatian women at the hands of their husbands as a result of the "never forgotten" propaganda about the value of dying Galatians? Remember "a good Galatian is a dying Galatian"? Women who suffered rape and enslavement as a result of being both women and Galatian would have likely received and interpreted Paul's letter differently from those who hadn't. Upon hearing it, the Galatian women very well could have re-experienced shame and

18. See Carolyn Osiek, "Galatians," in *Women's Bible Commentary*, ed. Carol A. Newsom, Sharon H. Ringe, and Jacqueline E. Lapsley (Louisville: Westminster John Knox, 2012); Beverly Roberts Gaventa, *Our Mother Saint Paul* (Louisville: Westminster John Knox, 2007).

19. Parker, "One Womanist's View," 32.

trauma. As I draw the lived experience of the Galatians into conversation with Black and minoritized bodies today, I would argue that critical engagement with Paul means contemporary readers must question Paul's characterization of himself as a mother and an enslaved person even though he did not have the lived experiences of either identity. It is almost as if Paul gaslights the Galatian women who may be hearing his letter and denies what their own particular lived reality actually entails.

While she doesn't use the language of "gaslighting," one scholar who helps me enter the text of Galatians is Jennifer Glancy. In her work Glancy addresses violence in the Roman imperial period while also specifically seeking to understand the Greek term for "body" (*sōma*) from a gendered view of violence as it relates to female bodies. Focusing on material bodies in early Christianity, Glancy notes that these bodies may be gendered bodies, alienated bodies, or bodies forced to succumb to physical or sexual violence, similar to the wife of the suicidal Gaul.[20] These bodies represent the lowest (or least privileged) bodies on the rungs of the Roman Empire. Interrogating the use of "slavery" and "oppression" in early Christianity as metaphors alone, Glancy expands previous scholarship by arguing against metaphorical bodies and focusing on actual bodies in the Greco-Roman age.[21] No longer can New Testament scholars disregard the abuse and violence that were ubiquitous during the reign of the Roman Empire and how these realities may have influenced the way gendered women heard

20. See Jennifer Glancy, *Slavery in Early Christianity* (Minneapolis: Fortress, 2006), 15–26. Glancy outlines what surrogate bodies, female bodies, sexual surrogates, and male bodies underwent in Roman imperial slavery.

21. Glancy, *Slavery*, 12. See also Dale B. Martin, *Slavery as Salvation: The Metaphor of Slavery in Pauline Christianity* (New Haven: Yale University Press, 1990). In his work Martin does not intend to "shed any great light on the narrative subject of the relation of early Christianity to slavery" but rather to uncover how scholars can explain the "positive, soteriological use of slavery as a symbol for the Christian's relationship to God or Christ" (xiv).

Paul's letter to the Galatian church. With that background, I can move to my translation and exegetical work on certain passages of Galatians, reading as an ethnic woman who would have been considered "other" from both a Roman perspective and a Jewish perspective in the Galatian context.

A Womanist Translation and Exegesis of Selected Galatians Texts

If I had to loosely outline all six chapters of the Galatians text, I would do so as follows:

I.   Greetings, Salutations, and Contextualization (1:1–5)
II. Paul's Defense of His Apostolic Calling and Ideas Concerning Faith (1:6–2:21)
III. The Law's Relationship to Faith (3:1–4:31)
IV. Freedom and Living by the Spirit (5:1–6:10)
V.   Conclusion (6:11–18)

In Galatians 1:1–5, the reader begins to understand Paul's characterization of himself and Jesus in relationship to the Galatians. I will argue that Paul primes the Galatians to "bond" with Jesus as one "raised from the dead." In Galatians 1:6–2:21, we begin to see Paul's differentiation of himself from Peter, Barnabas, and the rest of the Judaic sect who had come to teach the Galatian community. At this juncture I would argue that 2:15 is important for understanding what "make it home" actually means for a group like the Galatians, who had the cultural memory of being vanquished by Attalus's army. I will not cover Galatians 3–4, but I will examine Richard Hays's narrative structure through a Womanist lens. Finally, I will end with Paul's language of "bearing" to contend that "making it home" actually means looking out for one another, a central part of mature faith.

Galatians 1:1: Raised from the Dead Ones

Paul's letter to the Galatians begins with Paul immediately placing his apostolic credentials squarely in front of the Galatian people while also emphasizing that "God Father" is the one raising Jesus *ek nekrōn*. The traditional translation of *ek nekrōn* is "from the dead."[22] However, when I am teaching Galatians, I acknowledge that while most scholars focus on the apocalyptic dimensions of Galatians 1:1–5 and God's revelation though Jesus (which is important), I find it essential to enter the story from a Galatian viewpoint. Remember, I teach at a Baptist seminary where hardly any of my students are Jewish. Beginning from the positionality of the Galatians, therefore, seems highly appropriate.

The term *nekros*, found in the genitive plural in Galatians 1:1, was used frequently in the ancient world both as an adjective and as a substantive (a noun to represent a group of people). In our Western thought system, we often think of Jesus being raised from the dead—that is, from a physical state of being. When I read Galatians 1:1, I question whether "whom he raised from the dead" is a proper translation.

I would argue that Paul's use of a masculine, plural, genitive construction is a substantive use of *nekros*, which is not comparable to our Western understanding of being literally dead. According to the *Exegetical Dictionary of the New Testament*, which I agree with, a better translation would be "whom he raised from dead ones." I wonder if the Galatians, who had both men and women in their congregation, would have heard "dead men and women." I imagine the women would have included themselves in the opening salutations of the letter, even though later the lan-

22. K. Aland, B. Aland, J. Karavidopoulos, C. M. Martini, and B. M. Metzger, *Novum Testamentum Graece*, 28th ed. (Stuttgart: Deutsche Bibelgesellschaft, 2012).

guage shifts to circumcision, which would have been strictly for the men.

"From the dead ones" or even "from the dead men and women" gives a slightly different connotation than "from the no longer living." And it makes better sense in light of how the Galatians understood their identity in the Roman imperial context as "the only good Galatian is a dead Galatian."[23] Yes, God has raised Jesus as his Son, but Jesus has also been raised from the midst of dead women and men. Jesus, therefore, is the risen brother of the many dying and suicidal Galatians who have come before him. I find this thought liberating and hopeful, as Jesus is brother to many of us who may be in a state of dying as a result of imperial violence against our Black or minoritized bodies. Because Jesus rising from the dead is central to early Christian preaching, we have to remember to nuance and connect Jesus's rising to the narrative of the Galatian community.[24]

Faith in Christ versus Faith of Christ

After expressing his disgust with the "foolish" Galatians and with the hypocrisy of Peter that led astray Paul's stick buddy, Barnabas, Paul then moves to the idea of couching believers' faith in the faith of Jesus. The language of 2:16 is where Paul writes both, I argue, the subjective genitive and the objective genitive that I referenced earlier in this chapter. I have outlined three different translations—mine, the English Standard Version, and the New Revised Standard Version—in order to show slight differences and nuances.

---

23. H. R. Balz and G. Schneider, *Exegetical Dictionary of the New Testament* (Grand Rapids: Eerdmans, 1990), 2:459–61. I would also state that Kahl's reading of the Altar of Pergamon as being built on many dead ones is similar. See Kahl, *Galatians Re-Imagined*, 77–128.

24. D. C. Arichea and E. A. Nida, *A Handbook on Paul's Letter to the Galatians* (New York: United Bible Societies, 1976), 5–6.

But knowing that a person is not made just/right by
works of law
But through (the) **faith of Jesus Christ** (*pistis Iēsou
Christou*)
And we **believe in Christ Jesus** (*pisteuō eis
Christon*)
So that we may be made just/right by **(the) faith
of Christ** (*pistis Christou*)
And not works of law
Because no flesh will be made just by works of law.
(2:16, my translation)

Yet we know that a person is not justified by works of
the law
but through **faith in Jesus Christ**,
so we also have **believed in Christ Jesus**,
in order to be justified by **faith in Christ** and not by
works of the law,
because by works of the law no one will be justified.
(2:16 ESV)

Yet we know that a person is justified not by the
works of the law
but through **faith in Jesus Christ**.
And we have come to **believe in Christ Jesus**,
so that we might be justified by **faith in Christ**, and
not by doing the works of the law,
because no one will be justified by the works of the
law. (2:16 NRSV)

As you can see, I have a difficult time in my own translation deciding between "make just" or "make right" for the verb *dikaioō*.
There could be a connection to the idea of justice, but there could

also be an idea of things being set right. Regarding justice, most scholars, Hays included, believe there is some implication of forensic or judicial reckoning because of the connection to apocalyptic language in Galatians 1. That may be true, but I am undecided because I also believe that the expanded idea of faith could mean that part of being "made right" stems from our relationships with one another.

With that being said, I think that as translators we often do not give Paul (or even contemporary Bible readers) enough credit for the complexities that can occur within single words or phrases. Instead of trying to find the "one" correct interpretation, can't we live in the multiplicity of meaning where competing ideas can be equally valid and life-giving? I would argue that such uncertainties actually allow the mystery of God to shine through. Can we live in that mystery?

Additionally, I would contend that Paul addresses both subjective faith and objective faith in this one sentence. First, we can see that faith does not originate with the believer in Jesus but in Jesus himself. As I speak about God raising Jesus from the dead ones, I argue that Jesus had faith to believe that God would raise him from the dead ones. So, dear reader, what does it mean to think about Jesus being with both the actual dead and those who currently experience what it means to be vanquished? That is what I think the faith of Jesus alludes to.

Moreover, Paul still has enough wherewithal to center belief in Jesus. And this is where I think Paul moves from faith being a strictly mental, creedal, or intellectual act to it being an actual walk in which we all "make it home." I make this argument because Jesus, again, is raised not only from an inert state or some spiritual netherworld but also from those Galatians who are alive and yet experience vanquishing in their present. That means the dead ones (the Galatians) witnessed Jesus in the same state as them. Part of having the faith of Jesus as we all attempt to make it home means that we are in the same state as the ones we are walking home with. Again, this is not a creedal understanding of faith or an inerrant or infallible doctrine that is cut-and-dried. This is a messy doctrine because Jesus's faith unto God was messy as he walked along the way with crowds unto death.

We see this even in the Gospel of Mark. The Greek word *hodos* appears consistently as Jesus, the disciples, and the crowds walk along the *hodos*, or along the way. So in Mark 11:20–21 when Peter sees the fig tree that Jesus has cursed, Peter points out the tree to Jesus. What is interesting is that the same objective/subjective debate occurs in Mark 11:22, where Jesus literally says to Peter, "Have faith of God," even though most translations say, "Have faith in God." The point is that the Pauline text and even a snippet of the Mark text promote a nuanced understanding of what walking by the faith of the Son of God along the way actually entails. These snippets of being with others compels me to want to walk with everyone so that we all "make it home" by the faith of the Son of God.

Bearing Womanist Air unto Deep Faith

The final translation issues I will address stem from Paul's use of the Greek word *bastazō*, which translates into "bearing." In the latter half of Galatians, Paul uses the verb *bastazō* four times.[25] First, in Galatians 5:10, the ones identified as troubling the Galatians "will bear" judgment, in Paul's future apocalyptic understanding. Second, Paul exhorts the Jesus followers in Galatia to (presently) bear the burdens of one another so that they may fulfill the law of

---

25. My translation is as follows. Gal. 5:10: "I am confident about you in the Lord, that you will not think otherwise. But whoever it is that is stirring you up will bear the judgment." Gal. 6:2: "Bear one another's burdens, and thus you will fulfill the law of Christ" (present active imperative use of the verb).

Christ. Interestingly, the phrase "law of Christ" appears nowhere else in the New Testament. With that knowledge, I have to wonder how the "law of Christ" interacts with what Paul identifies as "works of law" in Galatians 2:16. In the context that I have already outlined, it would appear to me that the law of Christ may represent the notion of following Christ to the point where we resist our former identities as "dead men and women" by walking with one another to the point that we all make it home. So, too, each person remains distinct even as the community becomes one under the law of Christ. Third, in Galatians 6:5, Paul writes that each person "will bear" his own burden. Again, this future use of *bastazō* outlines Paul's apocalyptic idea that in future judgment, the Lord—not others in the community—will be the one to judge people's actions. Finally, Paul rounds out his usage of *bastazō* in Galatians 6:17 with another present-tense rendition as he talks about bearing Jesus's marks in his body.

These various uses of *bastazō* (future, present, future, and present tense, respectively) show how any present-tense use of "bearing" staves the idea of a negative future judgment. Specifically, I would argue that Paul's idea of "bearing with one another now" means "walking with one another" to the point that when the end is revealed, we will have done well enough to not worry about what "judgment" looks like. In essence, part of mature faith means walking (as I keep hammering) with one another so that we all "make it home." That is Womanist bearing and, I would add, mature faith.

Each future-tense use of *bastazō* connotes a negative concept of judgment for the one doing the bearing in the future, as opposed to the present-tense use of *bastazō*, which invokes the idea of a present transformation both within the Galatian community and in Paul's own body. For Paul, bearing the marks of Jesus in his body now is preferred to bearing judgment later, since it shows the transformation within Paul himself from a persecutor to a persecuted one. In that same vein, "bearing the burdens of one another" shows the transformation within the Galatian community while also showing the threat that transformation causes to the established imperial order. People who are bound together to bear one another's burdens are a stronger, cohesive community that can withstand many trials and warfare while continuing to grow in the faith and as persons of faith.

Maturing to Womanist "Bearing" Today

If we take Paul seriously, I believe that "bearing" unto a mature faith in which we all "make it home" is what a nuanced Womanist understanding of Galatians requires. Bearing with one another allows faith to develop across identities. If my oppressed identity has to walk alone to the point where I do not make it home and, instead of being my support, a "believer" performs microaggressive acts against me and continues to gaslight my reality, is that mature faith? These are among the questions we need to ask ourselves as we continue to read Galatians in a manner beyond the Lutheran ideal of "justification by faith alone."

Additionally, I believe that part of mature faith means that while we are reading Paul's language with nuance, we also recognize that he may not have women in mind as he writes to the Galatians. As I alluded to in this chapter, Paul does use women's bodies and experiences as he talks about being a birthing mother. I take issue with his privileged use and co-opting of women's bodies to make a theological point. While I recognize that Paul may use his privilege and, in turn, gaslight Galatian women out of their own experience, part of my mature faith means recognizing the theoretical framework of privilege that Paul engages even as I take issue, while still growing in mature faith because of his writings and not simply because they are deemed inerrant and infallible. Privilege means some groups benefit from unearned and unacknowledged advantages that increase their power in relationship to that of others. As a result, social inequality occurs. Generally invisible to others, multiple factors such as race, gender, age, sexual orientation, and class influence a person's level of privilege. In our contemporary society, privilege has many benefits, including access to housing, education, and jobs. Additionally, in the context of reading biblical texts in the midst of Black Lives Matter, privilege shows that while the majority of White US citizens do not expect to be killed by police while unarmed, Black and minoritized bodies have no such advantage, as protesters across the country recognize. Privilege also means that White women who suffer rape are more likely to be believed than Black women since perception in the United States still hypersexualizes Black women and views us as "legitimate victims." In essence, privilege endows Whites (men, mostly) with a sense of self-confidence and comfortableness that they experience without needing to think about said sense. Paul evidences his self-confidence and comfortableness in equating his identity with both an enslaved person and a birthing woman. These elements of privilege feed into White supremacist authoritarianism if we do not engage them as we read Pauline literature. In the context of all these understandings, mature faith must grow and endure so that we can become better faith communities that help each other "make it home."

Questions for Consideration

I have been a woman trying to get home from community college after a night class, only to get pulled over by the North Carolina State Police. This happened two to three times a semester on the same highway around the same time. I was driving a minivan and was often trying to get to my parents' house to pick up my children to go home. Many nights I would pray just to "make it home." At that time in my life, I did not realize that a Black woman driving a minivan after nine at night meant I "must have been smuggling drugs" on Capital Boulevard. We have seen a rise in recorded incidents between Black and minoritized bodies and the police where some end up dead. What we do not see are the Black and minoritized bodies that are traumatized because of constant harassment and pressure when we are just trying to "make it home." No question here—just an invitation to reflect on experiences that you remember in your body, and a reminder that when others open up in describing such experiences to you, to listen gently and affirm.

Conclusion:
Breathing Womanist Air

In his work, African American biblical scholar Vincent Wimbush engages the life and narrative of the formerly enslaved Olaudah Equiano. Wimbush mentions how even after the "White man" used the Bible against Africans, Equiano turned and used the Bible against the Miskito tribe of Central America.[1] In essence, Equiano became a wielder of the hegemony of Whiteness when he flashed the Bible as a magical fetish and an object of power. I identify Equiano as a person who engaged the Bible idolatrously. Waving the Bible in order to quell an uprising of the Miskito tribe and threatening severe and dire consequences should the Miskito Indians not disperse, Equiano recounts, "I told them God lived there, and he was angry with them . . . and if they did not leave off, and go away quietly, I would take the book, read, and tell God to make them dead."[2] Noting that Equiano admits his gesture is like magic, Wimbush argues that what would have been most disturbing to Equiano's readers was "the depiction of a nonwhite man actually performing the *authority of the white man*."[3] Wimbush's work is important to show that those of us who get close to the

1. Vincent L. Wimbush, *White Men's Magic: Scripturalization as Slavery* (New York: Oxford University Press, 2012).
2. Quoted in Wimbush, *White Men's Magic*, 154.
3. Wimbush, *White Men's Magic*, 178; emphasis added.

biblical text are not supposed to wield the Bible as a tool of White supremacist authoritarianism.

As a Womanist biblical scholar, I do not imagine my vocational call to include reading the biblical text in a White supremacist authoritarian way. In essence, that is what Equiano did when he used the Bible against the Miskito tribe. Instead, what I am called to do is to tell the Jesus story in such a way that it is not reduced to creedal ideas alone and to show that biblical authority is inspired breathing. It must move all folks who hold the biblical text as sacred to a nuanced engagement with the actual bodily experiences of people across all diversities.

If God Still Breathes, Why Can't I? reveals how White supremacist authoritarianism is often embedded in Christian notions of biblical authority, stifling God's breath. I wrote this "part memoir, part biblical scholarship" book with the understanding that the need to root out White supremacist authoritarianism from biblical interpretation is ever present in today's society and imagination because of all the various hardships and atrocities we are witnessing today. At the time of this writing, in the United States, close to 550,000 souls have been lost to COVID-19, protesters are still taking to the streets to march against police brutality aimed toward Black and minoritized bodies, wildfires are continuously burning on large acres of land on the West Coast, hurricanes are bombarding the southern shores of the southern states, and a riotous mob stormed the Capitol on January 6, 2021. Does a view of Scripture as inerrant and infallible allow us to even begin to imagine what liberation looks like in the midst of all these atrocities? What I have argued throughout this book is that ignoring the cultural issues within both the biblical text and our contemporary society will be detrimental to any type of survival on the planet Earth. The purpose of this book is to challenge marginalized biblical scholars and communities to move beyond the White supremacist authoritarianism of the doctrines of inerrancy and infallibility in order to envision a modicum of liberation in today's world.

I began in chapter 1 with the idea of engaging one's relationship to the biblical text. In every seminary course I have taught, I have begun by discussing my training as a biblical scholar and how many seminary programs train students to be "White male biblical scholars" even if their curricula are not explicit about that goal. To prepare to delve into issues regarding White supremacist authoritarianism and its connection to biblical authority, I began to lay the groundwork of how embodied identity comes to the forefront as biblical scholars ask questions of Scripture. Additionally, I showed how the issue of embodied identity can highlight how certain identities construct lenses for reading the Bible with or without connection to their own embodied identities.

In chapter 2, "White Supremacist Authoritarianism Is Not God's Breath," I pondered the idea of *auctoritas* and the fact that inherent to the meaning of "authority" is the concept of conversation, dialogue, and breath. The work of Seung Ai Yang, Ellen F. Davis, and Katie G. Cannon has been formative for these conversations. Moreover, I juxtaposed protective strategies that encircle evangelical views on the inerrancy and infallibility of Scripture with the Southern Strategy that caters to White Republican voters in the southern United States. This juxtaposition shows that there are groups of people (mainly White male interpreters of Scripture and political policy) who will go to great lengths to keep themselves in power.

In chapter 3, "Stop Gaslighting Me," I argued that doctrines become weapons of structural gaslighting in evangelical and mainline Protestant circles. I described how Black and minoritized bodies attempt to contort themselves to fit within evangelical circles, usually without success. Looking specifically at the concepts of microaggression, shame, and gaslighting, I argued that constant contortion into boxes that one does not fit in, or even wearing White masks over Black faces, is detrimental to one's psychological well-being. Shame ensues. I highlighted that other identities, even when "shamed" for particular stances, oftentimes do not exhibit shame because of the positions of power in which they dwell. This chapter ended with a thought experiment and interpretative moment wherein we read Mark 15:40–47 through the lens of gaslighting, seeing how the women who followed Jesus from Galilee in the Gospel of Mark were gazing upon men dwelling in power. Commentators still gaslight the women at the end of Mark by questioning their ability to be true disciples even though their womanhood was part of their following Jesus all the way to the tomb, whereas the male disciples left him.

In chapter 4, "Moving from Stifled Breath to Full-Throated Faith," I turned to Paul's letter to the Galatians to ponder mature faith formation, expanding the doctrinal idea of "faith in Jesus Christ" to "walking in the faith of Jesus Christ" unto death (that is, social death to White supremacist authoritarianism in faith communities). Engaging various readings of Galatians, I interpreted Galatians 2:16 as a call to "make it home" without holding our collective breath. Specifically, I argued that the idea of the "dying Gaul" in the context of the Galatians text lends itself to the comparison that just as "the only good Gaul is a dying Gaul," so too "the only good (fill in the blank) is a dead (fill in the blank)." When we think about Paul's letter to the Galatians with such an expanded and nuanced view, minoritized and oppressed peoples can ask different questions about "faith in Christ" and "the faith of Christ." I made the argument that while doctrinal faith in Christ may be necessary for salvation in a "hereafter," part of walking in the faith *of* Christ means walking with one another so that we all can make it home together. I do not "make it home" if my White sisters and brothers do not make it home. I also hope that my White sisters and brothers gain the capacity to feel the same about me.

Next Steps: "Re-membering" as Breathing Womanist Air

As I stated in the introduction, I am a Womanist Christian wife to a strong Black man, Victor. I am the daughter of Robert and Argie. I am the mother of Ebony and Saron. I am the grandmother of Essence and Zayden. I am also a professor of the New Testament. All these identities are a part of who I am as a Womanist New Testament biblical scholar. In this work, I am trying to breathe. The question remains: How does one become inspired in such a time as this? How does one not become mired in despair and melancholic feelings when many of us witness Black death almost daily and others in the world still wonder why people shout "Black Lives Matter!"? This book shows the necessity of not continuing to suffocate under White supremacist authoritarianism but actually moving into full Womanist air by claiming our own inspiration as we read the biblical text. Part of reclaiming this inspiration means realizing that part of what multiple identities *must* do is reclaim all the memories we have wanted to suppress in the history of these "United" States of America over the course of the last four hundred years.

"Re-membering" Identities

Black and minoritized scholars cannot do the work of exorcising White supremacist authoritarianism on their own. The work has to be done by all of us. Pastors, preachers, laypeople in the church. Gone are the days of "being nice" and expecting change to occur. There needs to be a re-membering of identity for our White brothers and sisters—a going back and picking up something that was lost.

One aspect of ministry that I talk to predominantly White churches and pastors about is the idea that the work I do is not for my liberation alone or even for Black bodies alone. My White colleagues, White pastors, White preachers, and White friends must fight for their liberation from the chains of their Whiteness. Identity as White is a constructed experience. Being White has denial and amnesia embedded in it. When immigrants entered the United States, we must remember that whole people groups became "whitened" as a way to distinguish their fates from that of Native Americans and Black people.[4] Re-membering White identity means engaging in social death to White supremacist authoritarianism as we all seek to make it home.

"Re-membering" Inspiration

My formulation of "Womanist air" is rooted in the concept of "God-breathed" (*theopneustos*) in 2 Timothy 3:16. Traditionally, when laypeople read 2 Timothy, many understand *theopneustos* as pertaining only to the writings of the Old and New Testaments. However, if we understand the importance of reading 2 Timothy in its cultural context, we will realize that our contemporary readings based on inerrancy and infallibility are *mis*readings. Second Timothy 3:16 was written before the texts of the New Testament were even canonized.

To begin to think about inspiration, I recommend the work of Craig Allert. Allert looks to the early church fathers with the unique question of "Did the early church view *only* the documents that went into the New Testament canon as inspired and those alone?"[5] Allert shows that the short answer is no. The early church had a long list of documents that they considered "inspired." As Allert investigates Irenaeus, Origen, Eusebius, and several other church fathers, two observations emerge. First, nowhere do these

4. Mary Watkins and Helene Shulman, *Toward Psychologies of Liberation* (London: Palgrave MacMillan, 2008), 169-70.
5. Craig D. Allert, *A High View of Scripture? The Authority of the Bible and the Formation of the New Testament Canon* (Grand Rapids: Baker Academic, 2007), 59.

fathers ever refer to an orthodox writing outside the New Testament as "noninspired." If a father considered a writing to be not inspired, he would use the language of "heretical" since the writing lay outside the community of faith.[6] Second, even as the fathers applied the concept of inspiration to many documents in the growing New Testament canon, they also ascribed inspiration to other texts. For example, both Clement and Ignatius viewed their own writings and works as inspired! After giving additional examples, such as Cappadocian father Gregory of Nyssa (ca. 330–ca. 395) and his brother Basil, Allert comes down on the opinion that the term *theopneustos* was used by the early church fathers to describe many works outside the "official" biblical canon. With such an understanding of inspiration, what is to stop other documents from being classified *theopneustos*? I often end my New Testament survey class with a combined reading of Revelation and the Rev. Dr. Martin Luther King Jr.'s "Letter from a Birmingham Jail." Just as the writer of Revelation, I would argue, is trying to figure out how the early Jesus community can be considered human under the Roman imperial regime, Dr. King writes to his fellow clergymen who question why he left Atlanta to go to Birmingham. Dr. King responds that injustice in Birmingham demanded direct action. Specifically, Dr. King notes that freedom is never given voluntarily by the oppressor and then proceeds to quote Revelation and the lukewarm nature of many clergymen.

Dr. King's letter is an excellent example of continued inspiration today. His identity as an embodied Black man witnessing and undergoing severe injustices was a tool for his interpretation of the biblical text. Moreover, his interpretation was counter to that of many of the moderates who advised him to slow down. It is especially disheartening to witness scholars such as Greg Lukianoff and Jonathan Haidt invoking the memory of Dr. King to ar-

6. Allert, *High View of Scripture?*, 60.

gue *against* the importance of identity for oppressed communities. I would argue that inspiration comes from embracing the various identities within both the biblical text and the world around us in order to fight with and for one another for justice in a world that seems to be going horribly wrong.

Inspiration is a moment for all of us to breathe God's breath. Just as the biblical text inspires and points me to God, I must be an inspiration who inspires and points people to God and to one another. Scripture gives us permission to inspire, so I ask you, dear reader: Are you *mired* or *inspired*?

As I have argued, the doctrines of inerrancy and infallibility as tools of White supremacist authoritarianism do not liberate. They bring about microaggression and gaslighting. There is no way that living under such an oppressive system can bring anything but shame, harm, and ongoing trauma. As a Womanist biblical scholar, my call is to perform biblical interpretation not like a White male biblical scholar but, rather, in a way that provides flashes of table turning and table expansion. I seek to be a vessel and tool of inspiration for more people to read biblical texts more freely. I hope for an open table that is not owned by anyone and that has space for all.

AIR: Accept. Interrogate. Read Womanists!

So as we all set out to inspire, I will close this book with a short acronym to help you remember some main points and next steps. As a traditional three-point Baptist preacher, it seems appropriate to end with three points stemming from the acronym AIR.

First, *A*. The letter *A* stands for acceptance. Dear reader, please accept that you cannot know everything about the biblical text. You can also accept that while inerrancy and infallibility may have been useful doctrines in the past (although I doubt it), they are very limiting for engagement with the historical contexts and cultural complexities of the biblical text and for today's contemporary conversations. Accept that inerrancy and infallibility are often used as tools of complementarianism and slavery, placing members of society in a hierarchical system.

Next, the letter *I*. *I* stands for interrogation. Please, please, please interrogate your own various identities. Not everyone appreciates identity politics. However, if we humbly pay attention to where many of us stand in relationship to power, we may see that we are on a sliding scale of privilege. I often tell my students that when I am in the classroom, I am known as Dr. Parker. However, when I leave the "safety" of institutional buildings and stand outside at a bus stop, I am sometimes called the N-word by racist people. Part of my interrogation means noting my own sliding scale of privilege and how that slide up or down affects the way I read biblical texts.

Moreover, the deep interrogative work of biblical scholarship and its relationship to identity cannot be done by Black and minoritized scholars alone. Just as I bring my Womanist identity with me in biblical interpretation, the best way forward for liberation in biblical studies is for all of us, even our White scholars, to interrogate our own lived experience.

Finally, the letter *R*. *R* stands for the imperative to "Read Womanists!" Study with Womanists! Learn from Womanists! Compensate Womanists! There are many active Womanist biblical scholars who can broaden your interpretation of the biblical text; see the appendix for a list of names.

* * *

My hope, dear reader, is that this book, written unashamedly by a Womanist New Testament scholar, has ushered you into the potential of experiencing God's breath intermingling with your breath for justice and liberation. As I have stated previously, I love and respect the Bible, which is precisely why I'm so committed to wrestling with it and why I hate to see it used without thoughtful or critical reflection unto deep Womanist AIR. In this book I have questioned the doctrines of inerrancy and infallibility unto White supremacist authoritarianism and have found them lacking in sustaining inspired breathing. Even though I sometimes feel these doctrines rise up within my body (and you may also experience those tendencies from time to time), I promise to continue fighting against such tendencies so that I can excise them from any biblical interpretations I perform in the context of my communities. I hope you will do the same and let the real work of dismantling White supremacist authoritarianism begin!

Appendix

While this is not an exclusive list of Womanist biblical scholars, it will get you started in compiling a vast collection of Womanist works: Dr. Clarice P. Martin, Dr. Renita Weems, Dr. Mitzi Smith, Dr. Valerie Bridgeman, Dr. Wilda Gafney, Dr. Kimberly Russaw, Dr. Shanell Smith, Dr. Shively T. J. Smith, Dr. Bridgett Green, Dr. Vanessa Lovelace, Dr. Stephanie Buchanan Crowder, Dr. Cheryl Anderson, Dr. Febbie Dickerson, Dr. Love Sechrest, Dr. Marlene Underwood, Dr. Gay Byron, Dr. Stacy Davis, Dr. Lisa Bowens, Rev. Dr. Raquel Lettisome, Dr. Ericka Dunbar, Rev. Dr. Madeline McClenney-Sadler, Rev. Kamilah Hall Sharp, Minenhle Nomalungelo Khumalo, and Rev. Yolanda Norton. I also recommend the works of Dr. Margaret Aymer, Dr. Jennifer Kaalund, and Dr. Nyasha Junior as women who contribute to Womanist biblical interpretation but may not specifically identify as Womanist. I also ask that you read the work of our late Womanist sister Dr. Lynne St. Clair Darden. For international South African Womanist readings, please engage the work of Dr. Madipoane Masenya at the University of South Africa.

Finally, as we say in the Black church tradition, "If I have omitted anyone, please charge it to my head and not to my heart." This list comprises biblical scholars who have pursued or who are pursuing a PhD in Hebrew or New Testament. There also many talented Womanist theologians, such as Dr. Chanequa Walker-Barnes, not to mention the vast array of talented, gifted, and inspiring Womanist preachers and laypeople outside academia, all across the globe!

Bibliography

Alcoff, Linda Martin. *Visible Identities: Race, Gender, and the Self.* New York: Oxford University Press, 2006.

Allert, Craig D. *A High View of Scripture? The Authority of the Bible and the Formation of the New Testament Canon.* Grand Rapids: Baker Academic, 2007.

Arichea, D. C., and E. A. Nida. *A Handbook on Paul's Letter to the Galatians.* New York: United Bible Societies, 1976.

Bailey, Randall C. "We Shall Become White as Snow: When Bad Is Turned into Good." *Semeia* 76 (December 1998): 99–113.

Balz, H. R., and G. Schneider. *Exegetical Dictionary of the New Testament*, vol. 2. Grand Rapids: Eerdmans, 1990.

Benson, Bruce Ellis, Malinga Elizabeth Berry, and Peter Goodwin Heltzel, eds. *Prophetic Evangelicals: Envisioning a Just and Peaceable Kingdom.* Grand Rapids: Eerdmans, 2012.

Brown, Austin Channing. *I'm Still Here: Black Dignity in a World Made for Whiteness.* New York: Crown/Convergent, 2018.

Brown, Jessica Autumn. "The New 'Southern' Strategy." *Geopolitics, History, and International Relations* 8, no. 2 (2016): 22–41.

Brown, Raymond E. *Death of the Messiah: From Gethsemane to the Grave; A Commentary on the Passion Narratives in the Four Gospels.* New York: Doubleday, 1994.

Brown, William P., ed. *Engaging Biblical Authority: Perspectives on the Bible as Scripture.* Louisville: Westminster John Knox, 2007.

Bruce, F. F. *The Epistle to the Galatians: A Commentary on the Greek Text*. Grand Rapids: Eerdmans, 1982.

Campbell, Colin. "Trump: If I'm President, 'Christianity Will Have Power' in the US." *Business Insider*, January 23, 2016. https://www.businessinsider.com/donald-trump-christianity-merry -christmas-2016-1.

Cannon, Katie Geneva. "The Biblical Mainstay of Liberation." Pages 18–26 in *Engaging Biblical Authority*, edited by William P. Brown. Louisville: Westminster John Knox, 2007.

———. "The Emergence of Black Feminist Consciousness." Pages 30–40 in *Feminist Interpretation of the Bible*, edited by Letty M. Russell. Philadelphia: Westminster, 1985.

———. "Sexing Black Women: Liberation from the Prison house of Anatomical Authority." Pages 11–30 in *Loving the Body: Black Religious Studies and the Erotic*, edited by Anthony B. Pinn and Dwight N. Hopkins. New York: Palgrave Macmillan, 2004.

Cobb, Laurel K. *Mark and Empire: Feminist Reflections*. Maryknoll, NY: Orbis, 2013.

Collins, Patricia Hill. *Black Feminist Thought: Knowledge, Consciousness, and the Politics of Empowerment*. New York: Routledge, 2000.

———. *Intersectionality as Critical Social Theory*. Durham, NC: Duke University Press, 2019.

Cone, James H. *The Cross and the Lynching Tree*. Maryknoll, NY: Orbis, 2011.

———. *Said I Wasn't Gonna Tell Nobody: The Making of a Black Theologian*. Maryknoll, NY: Orbis, 2018.

Copeland, M. Shawn. "Body, Representation, and Black Religious Discourse." Pages 98–112 in *Womanist Theological Ethics: A Reader*, edited by Katie Geneva Cannon, Emilie M. Townes, and Angela D. Sims. Louisville: Westminster John Knox, 2011.

———. *Enfleshing Freedom: Body, Race, and Being*. Minneapolis: Fortress, 2008.

Davis, Ellen F. "The Soil That Is Scripture." Pages 36–44 in *Engaging Biblical Authority*, edited by William P. Brown. Louisville: Westminster John Knox, 2007.

DeMoss, M. S. *Pocket Dictionary for the Study of New Testament Greek.* Downers Grove, IL: InterVarsity, 2001.

Douglas, Kelly Brown. *Sexuality and the Black Church.* Maryknoll, NY: Orbis, 1999.

———. *What's Faith Got to Do with It? Black Bodies/Christian Souls.* Maryknoll, NY: Orbis, 2005.

Fatima, Saba. "I Know What Happened to Me: The Epistemic Harms of Microaggression." Pages 163–83 in *Microaggressions and Philosophy*, edited by Lauren Freeman and Jeanine Weekes Schroer. New York: Taylor & Francis Group, 2020.

Floyd-Thomas, Stacy M., ed. *Deeper Shades of Womanism in Religion and Society.* New York: New York University Press, 2006.

Gafney, Wilda C. *Womanist Midrash: A Reintroduction to the Women of the Torah and the Throne.* Louisville: Presbyterian Publishing, 2017.

Gaventa, Beverly Roberts. *Our Mother Saint Paul.* Louisville: Westminster John Knox, 2007.

Glancy, Jennifer. *Slavery in Early Christianity.* Minneapolis: Fortress, 2006.

Gundry, Robert H. *Mark: A Commentary on His Apology for the Cross.* Grand Rapids: Eerdmans, 1993.

Hare, Douglas R. A. *Mark.* Louisville: Westminster John Knox, 1996.

Harris-Perry, Melissa. *Sister Citizen: Shame, Stereotypes, and Black Women in America.* New Haven: Yale University Press, 2011.

Harvey, Jennifer. *Dear White Christians: For Those Still Longing for Racial Reconciliation.* Grand Rapids: Eerdmans, 2014.

Hays, Richard B. *The Faith of Jesus Christ: The Narrative Substructure of Galatians 3:1–4:11.* 2nd ed. Grand Rapids: Eerdmans, 2002.

Hooker, Morna D. *The Gospel according to Mark.* London: A & C Black, 1991.

Horowitz, Roger. *Kosher USA: How Coke Became Kosher and Other Tales of Modern Food*. New York: Columbia University Press, 2016.

Horrell, David G. *Ethnicity and Inclusion: Religion, Race, and Whiteness in Constructions of Jewish and Christian Identities*. Grand Rapids: Eerdmans, 2020.

Horsley, Richard A. *Hearing the Whole Story: The Politics of Plot in Mark's Gospel*. Louisville: Westminster John Knox, 2001.

Jacobs, Harriet A. *Incidents in the Life of a Slave Girl: Written by Herself*. Edited by Jean Fagan Yellin. 1861; repr. Cambridge, MA: Harvard University Press, 1998.

Jennings, Theodore W., Jr. *The Insurrection of the Crucified: The 'Gospel of Mark' as Theological Manifesto*. Chicago: Exploration Press, 2003.

Jernegan, Prescott F. "The Faith of Jesus Christ." *The Biblical World* 8, no. 3 (September 1896): 198–202.

Joshel, Sandra. "Nurturing the Master's Child: Slavery and the Roman Child-Nurse." *Signs* 12, no. 1 (Fall 1986): 3–22.

Junior, Nyasha. *An Introduction to Womanist Biblical Interpretation*. Louisville: Westminster John Knox, 2015.

Just, Arthur A. "The Faith of Christ: A Lutheran Appropriation of Richard L. Hays's Proposal." *Concordia Theological Quarterly* 70 (2006): 3–15.

Kahl, Brigitte. *Galatians Re-Imagined: Reading with the Eyes of the Vanquished*. Paul in Critical Contexts. Minneapolis: Fortress, 2010.

Kelley, Shawn. *Racializing Jesus: Race, Ideology and the Formation of Modern Biblical Scholarship*. New York: Routledge, 2002.

Kim, Seong Hee. *Mark, Women and Empire: A Korean Postcolonial Perspective*. Sheffield: Sheffield Phoenix Press, 2010.

Kinukawa, Hisako. *Women and Jesus in Mark: A Japanese Feminist Perspective*. Maryknoll, NY: Orbis, 1994.

Kugler, R. A., and P. J. Hartin. *An Introduction to the Bible*. Grand Rapids: Eerdmans, 2009.

Lancaster, Sarah Heaner. *Women and the Authority of Scripture: A Narrative Approach.* Harrisburg, PA: Trinity Press International, 2002.

Lee, Morgan. "John MacArthur Is No Stranger to Controversy: A Closer Look at the Ministry and Theology behind the Outspoken California Pastor." *Christianity Today*, October 23, 2019. https://www.christianitytoday.com/ct/2019/october-web-only/john-macarthur-beth-moore-controversy.html.

Lomax, Tamura. *Jezebel Unhinged: Loosing the Black Female Body in Religion and Culture.* Durham, NC: Duke University Press, 2008.

Lopez, Davina. *Apostle to the Conquered: Reimagining Paul's Mission.* Paul in Critical Contexts. Minneapolis: Fortress, 2009.

Lukianoff, Greg, and Jonathan Haidt. *The Coddling of the American Mind: How Good Intentions and Bad Ideas Are Setting Up a Generation for Failure.* New York: Penguin, 2018.

Malbon, Elizabeth Struthers. "Fallible Followers: Women and Men in the Gospel of Mark." *Semeia* 28 (1983): 29–48.

Malley, Brian. *How the Bible Works: An Anthropological Study of Evangelical Biblicism.* New York: AltaMira Press, 2004.

Marcus, Joel. *Mark 8–16: A New Translation with Introduction and Commentary.* New Haven: Yale University Press, 2009.

Martin, Clarice J. "The Haustafeln (Household Codes) in African American Biblical Interpretation: 'Free Slaves' and 'Subordinate Women.'" Pages 206–31 in *Stony the Road We Trod: African American Biblical Interpretation*, edited by Cain Hope Felder. Minneapolis: Fortress, 1991.

———. "Womanist Interpretations of the New Testament: The Quest for Holistic and Inclusive Translation and Interpretation." *Journal of Feminist Studies in Religion* 6, no. 2 (Fall 1990): 41–61.

Martin, Dale B. *Slavery as Salvation: The Metaphor of Slavery in Pauline Christianity.* New Haven: Yale University Press, 1990.

Maxwell, Angie, and Todd Shields. *The Long Southern Strategy: How Chasing White Voters in the South Changed American Politics.* New York: Oxford University Press, 2019.

McCaulley, Esau. *Reading While Black: African American Biblical Interpretation as an Exercise in Hope.* Downers Grove, IL: InterVarsity, 2020.

Miller, Susan. *Women in Mark's Gospel.* New York: T&T Clark International, 2004.

Mitchell, Joan L. *Beyond Fear and Silence: A Feminist-Literary Reading of Mark.* New York: Continuum, 2001.

Mitchem, Stephanie Y. *Introducing Womanist Theology.* Maryknoll, NY: Orbis, 2006.

Munro, Winsome. "Women Disciples in Mark?" *Catholic Bibilical Quarterly* 44 (1982): 225–41.

Myers, Ched. *Binding the Strong Man: A Political Reading of Mark's Story of Jesus.* Maryknoll, NY: Orbis, 1994.

Osiek, Carolyn. "Galatians." Pages 827–34 in *Women's Bible Commentary,* edited by Carol A. Newsom, Sharon H. Ringe, and Jacqueline E. Lapsley. Louisville: Westminster John Knox, 2012.

Parker, Angela N. "One Womanist's View of Racial Reconciliation in Galatians." *Journal of Feminist Studies in Religion* 34, no. 2 (October 1, 2018): 23–40.

———. "Reading Mary Magdalene with Stacey Abrams." Pages 155–70 in *Come and Read: Interpretative Approaches in the Gospel of John,* edited by Alicia D. Myers and Lindsey S. Jodrey. Lanham, MD: Lexington Books/Fortress Academic, 2019.

Patzia, A. G., and A. J. Petrotta. *Pocket Dictionary of Biblical Studies.* Downers Grove, IL: InterVarsity, 2002.

Pippin, Tina. "Translation Happens: A Feminist Perspective on Translation Theories." Pages 163–76 in *Escaping Eden: New Feminist Perspectives on the Bible,* edited by Harold C. Washington, Susan Lochrie Graham, and Pamela Thimmes. New York: New York University Press, 1999.

Sanders, E. P. *Paul and Palestinian Judaism.* Minneapolis: Fortress, 1977.

Schüssler Fiorenza, Elisabeth. *In Memory of Her: A Feminist Theological Reconstruction of Christian Origins.* 10th anniv. ed. New York: Herder & Herder, 1994.

Small, Pamela Felder, Marco J. Barker, and Marybeth Gasman, eds. *Sankofa: African American Perspectives on Race and Culture in US Doctoral Education.* Albany: State University of New York Press, 2020.

Taylor, Keeanga-Yamahtta. *From #BlackLivesMatter to Black Liberation.* Chicago: Haymarket Books, 2016.

Townes, Emilie. *Womanist Ethics and the Cultural Production of Evil.* Gordonsville, VA: Palgrave Macmillan, 2006.

Walker, Alice. *In Search of Our Mothers' Gardens.* New York: Harcourt Brace Jovanovich, 1983.

Walker-Barnes, Chanequa. *I Bring the Voices of My People: A Womanist Vision of Racial Reconciliation.* Grand Rapids: Eerdmans, 2019.

Weed, Eric. *The Religion of White Supremacy in the United States.* Lanham, MD: Lexington Books, 2017.

Weems, Renita. "Womanist Reflections on Biblical Hermeneutics." Pages 216–24 in *Black Theology: A Documentary History.* Vol. 2, *1980-1992*, edited by James H. Cone and Gayraud S. Wilmore. Maryknoll, NY: Orbis, 1993.

West, Traci C. "Spirit-Colonizing Violations: Racism, Sexual Violence and Black American Women." Pages 19–30 in *Remembering Conquest: Feminist/Womanist Perspectives on Religion, Colonization, and Sexual Violence*, edited by Nantawan Boonprasat Lewis and Marie M. Fortune. New York: Haworth, 1999.

Williams, Delores S. *Sisters in the Wilderness: The Challenge of Womanist God-Talk.* Maryknoll, NY: Orbis, 2013.

Yang, Seung Ai. "The Word of Creative Love, Peace, and Justice." Pages 132–40 in *Engaging Biblical Authority: Perspectives on the Bible as Scripture*, edited by William P. Brown. Louisville: Westminster John Knox, 2007.

Young, Stephen L. "Protective Strategies and the Prestige of the 'Academic': A Religious Studies and Practice Theory Redescription of Evangelical Inerrantist Scholarship," *Biblical Interpretation* 23 (2015): 1–35.

Index

Note: Page numbers followed by "*f*" indicate figures.

Abrams, Stacey, 40
acceptance, 98–99
activism and resistance, 53–54, 55
"activist translation," 66
AIR (acceptance, interrogation,
    reading Womanists), 98–99
Alcoff, Linda Martin, 20
Allert, Craig, 40, 41, 96–97
assimilation, 55
Attalus I, 75, 77
auctoritas, 26–27, 93
Augustine of Hippo, 23–24
authoritarianism, 6–7, 9, 31–32.
    See also biblical authoritar-
    ianism; White supremacist
    authoritarianism
authority. *See also* biblical authority
    etymology of, 26–27
    misuses of, 6–7, 9, 31–32

Bailey, Randall, 67–68
Barrett, Amy Coney, 46
bastazō, 85–87
Baur, Ferdinand Christian, 15, 16
Beyond Fear and Silence (Mitchell),
    58n19
biblical authoritarianism, 7n4, 11,

30, 34–37, 74. *See also* biblical
    interpretation, White suprema-
    cist authoritarianism in
biblical authority
    vs. biblical authoritarianism, 7n4,
        35–36
    vs. idolatry, 28–29
    as inspired breathing, 27–28, 92,
        93
    origin of, 30–31
    vs. White supremacist authoritar-
        ianism, 4, 6, 28, 30–31, 53, 92
biblical interpretation, White su-
    premacist authoritarianism in
    vs. biblical authority, 4, 6, 28,
        30–31, 53, 92
    bibliolatry as form of, 30
    cultural components of, 41–42
    decentering/excising, 5, 9, 11, 63,
        70, 92, 94, 95–96
    defensiveness around, 1–2, 8, 9
    Eurocentric perspectives as-
        sumed in, 16–17, 19, 31, 71
    forced consistency of, 34, 74
    of Galatians, 71–72, 73
    identity and, 24, 40, 52, 68

inerrancy/infallibility doctrines
and, 7, 32, 41-42, 44
of Mark, 57-58, 61-62
mature interpretation hindered
by, 28, 31, 34, 74, 96
by nonwhite Christians, 91-92
objectivity associated with,
19-20
political display of, 4, 31-32, 36,
40, 46, 93
power and privilege associated
with, 6, 88
protective strategies, 32, 33-37,
39, 40-42, 93
psychological components of, 42,
44, 46, 61
racism dialogue shaped by, 5, 55
in seminary training, 14-15, 19,
31, 33, 52, 93
by students, 1-2
term usage, 6-7, 26
translation and, 66-67
biblical interpretation, Womanist
critical consciousness in, 37
embodied identity and, 24, 93, 97
faith formation and, 28, 37
intersectionality and, 54-55
lived experience and, 52-53
purposes of, 20-21
regaining breath through, 3,
17-18, 20, 56-61, 95
tools in, 53, 54-55
writers' intentionality and, 57-58
biblical scholarship, White
male-dominated, 13-15, 19, 31,
33, 52
biblical scholarship, Womanist
embodied perspective of, 4, 20,
22-23, 40, 52, 70
fear factors associated with, 38
identity interrogated in, 53, 99
impact of, 18, 24, 95-96

interpretive tools in, 53, 54-55
lived experience in, 15
purposes of, 20-21
reading and engaging with, 99
vs. stifled breath, 17-18
translation theory and, 65-67, 70
bibliolatry, 29-30
"Black Feminist Consciousness,
The" (Cannon), 20
Black Feminist Thought (Collins), 53
Black Jezebel image, 22
Black Lives Matter movement,
4n2, 88
blepō, 58
bodies, Black female
contorted in evangelical spaces,
11, 44, 51-52, 93
devalued and hypersexualized,
22-23, 88
gendered violence against,
79-80
identity connected to, 22
boundaries, denominational, 42
breath, factors stifling. See also
biblical interpretation, White
supremacist authoritarianism
in; inerrancy and infallibility,
doctrines of
Eurocentric-oriented scholarship, 14-15, 19, 31, 33, 52
objectivity, 19-20, 69
police violence, 2-3
protective strategies, 33-37, 39,
40-42, 93
structural gaslighting, 11, 49-53
breath, of God, 2, 10, 12, 53, 92,
96, 98
breath, stifled, 17
breath, strategies for regaining. See
also faith formation
critical social theory, 53-55

identity and relationality, 19,
  20, 28
intersectionality, 54–55
re-membering, 95–99
Sankofa moments, 55–56
Womanist biblical interpretation,
  3, 17–18, 20, 56–61, 95
Brown, Austin Channing, 51
Brown, William, 27
Buddhism, 29–30
Bultmann, Rudolf, 73
burdens, bearing, 63, 85–87

Calvin, John, 8
Campbell, Douglas, 70, 72
Cannon, Katie Geneva, 20, 31, 93
Celtic spirituality, 75n16
class, 65–66
Clement, 97
Coddling of the American Mind, The
  (Lukianoff, Haidt), 47–48
Collins, Patricia Hill, 53–55
"color blindness," 55
communalism, traditional, 21
Cooper, Amy, 9
Cooper, Christian, 9
Cooperative Baptist Fellowship, 33
Copeland, M. Shawn, 22
Copher, Charles, 67
critical engagement, 21, 37
critical theories, 40–41, 53–55

Davis, Ellen, 13, 36–37, 93
"dead men and women"/"dead
  ones," 81–82, 84, 86
Democratic Party, 39–40
denominational statements, 42
dikaioō translation, 83–84
doctrine. *See* inerrancy and infallibility, doctrines of
Douglas, Kelly Brown, 22–23
doulos translation, 67

Duke Divinity School, 14–15, 19
Dying Gaul, The, 74f, 75–76, 77, 94

ek nekrōn translation, 81
Elliot, Elizabeth, 51
Equiano, Olaudah, 91, 92
evangelicals, White, 6, 33–37, 39,
  40–42, 93
Evangelical Theological Society,
  34, 35, 37, 39

faith, justification by, 71n12, 76
faith formation
  across identities, 87
  Bible reading approaches for,
    28–32, 37
  vs. certainty, 28, 65, 70–71
  "faith in Jesus Christ" *vs.* "walk-
    ing in the faith of Jesus," 63,
    82–87, 92, 94
  hindered by inerrancy and
    infallibility doctrines, 34, 71–73,
    74, 96
  hindered by White supremacist
    authoritarianism, 28, 31, 34,
    74, 96
  re-membering and, 95–99
Faith of Jesus Christ, The (Hays), 72
Fatima, Saba, 47, 48, 50
feminism, 20, 21, 38, 39
Floyd, George, 2, 49
Foucault, Michele, 59–60
fundamentalism, Christian, 34, 39

Gafney, Wilda, 67, 68–69
Galatians, book of
  certainty *vs.* tension in, 65, 73
  context for, 71–72, 75
  "make it home" theme in, 63, 72,
    80, 84, 86, 94
  Paul's self-identification, 77–79,
    80

pistis Iēsou Christou translation, 72–73
visual imagery and, 74f, 75–76, 77, 94
"walking by the faith of Jesus the Christ" in, 72, 84–85, 86, 94
White supremacist authoritarian reading of, 71–72, 73
Womanist translation/exegesis of, 65, 70–71, 80–88
Garland, Merrick, 46
gaslighting
  in biblical interpretation, 52, 61–62, 87
  in Christian institutions and culture, 49–53
  defined, 49, 50
  minority identities erased by, 52, 87
  psychological consequences of, 93–94
  via inerrancy and infallibility doctrines, 11, 44, 49–51, 61–62, 98
Gaul Killing Himself and His Wife, 76f
Gauls, Celtic, 75
Gaventa, Beverly Roberts, 77–78
"gazing," 58–60, 94
gender
  in biblical interpretation, 60–61
  in biblical translation, 10n5, 65–66
  in hearing of Scripture, 79–80
  roles, 39
Ginsburg, Ruth Bader, 46
Glancy, Jennifer, 79
Gramsci, Antonio, 40, 41
Grant, Jacquelyn, 21
Gregory of Nyssa, 97
Gundry, Robert, 34–35, 37, 39, 40

Hagar, 78
Haidt, Jonathan, 47–48, 97–98
Harris-Perry, Melissa, 45, 46
Hays, Richard, 14, 70, 72–74, 83
Hegel, G. W. F., 16–17
hegemony, cultural, 40–42
historical-critical method, 19, 24, 52–53
hodos, 85
Holy Spirit, 30–31
Horrell, David, 15, 16
household codes, 39

identity/identities
  in biblical interpretation, 24, 40, 52–53, 97
  in biblical scholarship, 52, 75–76, 82, 93
  in biblical translation, 66–67
  defined, 20
  embodied nature of, 22
  interrogating, 99
  mature and renewed, 86, 87
  minoritized, 47
  relationships and, 19, 20, 28
  re-membering, 95–96
  shame and, 47, 94
  White, 96
  White supremacist authoritarianism and, 24, 40, 52, 68
  Womanist, 19–21, 22
identity politics, 48, 97–98
Ignatius, 97
I'm Still Here (Brown), 51
inerrancy and infallibility, doctrines of
  authority tied to, 9
  bibliolatry and, 30
  blind spots and, 54
  communal memory erased by, 3, 80, 82, 86–87

cultural and psychological components of, 41–42
defined, 7–8
experience of God's breath stifled by, 4, 10–12, 98
gaslighting via, 11, 44, 49–51, 61–62, 98
individual salvation tied to, 45
maturing hindered by, 34, 71–73, 74, 96
microaggression and shame through, 45, 98
protective strategies around, 33–37, 39, 40–42, 93
purpose of, 32–33
racial dialogue shaped by, 55
resistance to questioning, 1–3, 8, 9
term usage, 7–8
as tool of control, 33, 34, 53–54, 74, 98
translation and, 68
White supremacist authoritarianism and, 7, 32, 41–42, 44
In Memory of Her (Schüssler Fiorenza), 58n19
inspiration, 9–10, 65, 96–98
interrogation, 99
intersectionality, 53, 54–55
Intersectionality as Critical Social Theory (Collins), 54

Jesus Christ, 15–17, 63, 82–87, 92, 94
Jezebel image, 22
Joseph of Arimathea, 60–61
Josephus, 57
Journal for Feminist Studies in Religion, 18
judgment, 86
justice (term usage), 10

Kahl, Brigitte, 75
Kelley, Shawn, 15, 16
Kemp, Brian, 40
Kim, Seong Hee, 58n19
King, Martin Luther, Jr., 97–98
Kinukawa, Hisako, 58n19

"law of Christ," 86
"Letter from a Birmingham Jail" (King), 97
liberation, 92–93, 95–96, 98, 99
Long Southern Strategy, The (Maxwell, Shields), 38
Lopez, Davina, 75
Ludovisi Gaul (Suicidal Gaul), 75, 76f, 77
Lukianoff, Greg, 47–48, 97–98
Luther, Martin, 8, 71n12

MacArthur, John, 35–37
"Make It Home" (Nwigwe), 63
"make it home" theme
  in Galatians, 63, 72, 80, 84, 86, 94
  issues propelling, 63, 92
  personal experience, 88–89
Malley, Brian, 42
Marcus, Joel, 14
Mark, Gospel of
  "gazing" in, 59–60, 94
  historical context for, 56–57
  inerrant/infallible readings of, 57–58, 61–62
  oral transmission of, 57n17
  through gaslighting lens, 56–58, 94
  "walking by the faith of Jesus the Christ" in, 85
  Womanist reading of, 56–59, 94
Mark, Women, and Empire (Kim), 58n19
Martin, Clarice, 66–67

Martin, Dale, 79n21
Marxism, 40, 41
maturity. *See* faith formation
Maxwell, Angie, 38, 39, 40
microaggression
  in biblical interpretation, 61
  defined, 44-45
  dialogue about, 45, 47-49
  impact of, 47, 51-52, 93-94
  power and, 60
midrash, rabbinic, 34, 35
Miller, Susan, 58n19
Miskito tribe, 91, 92
Mitchell, Joan L., 58n19
Moore, Beth, 35
Myers, Ched, 61n23

nekros, 81
Nwigwe, Tobe, 63

Obama, Barack, 46
objective genitive, 72-73
objectivity, 19-20, 24, 69
Osiek, Caroline, 77-78

Paul. *See also* Galatians, book of
  diverse audiences and contexts
    of, 74
  faith in Jesus *vs.* of Jesus, 82-84
  scholarly approaches to, 71n12
  self-identification of, 77-79, 87,
    88
  transformation of, 86-87
Pippin, Tina, 65-66, 69
pistis Iēsou Christou, 72-73, 74,
  82-83
pneuma, 31n4
power. *See also* White supremacist
    authoritarianism
  biblical authoritarianism and,
    35-37
  biblical justification of, 18

confronting and regaining, 36,
  53-56
evangelical defense of, 33-37, 39,
  40-42, 93
"gaze" and, 60
identity and, 94, 99
privilege, 87-88, 99
protective strategies, 32, 33-37, 39,
  40-42, 93
Proudfoot, Wayne, 33-34

race and racism, 5, 53, 55, 65-68
Reagan, Ronald, 38
relationships, 19, 20, 28
re-membering, 11, 27, 95-99
Republican Party, 38, 39-40, 46, 93
righteousness, 10
Rini, Regina, 48, 49
Roman Empire, 55, 56, 71n12, 72,
  75, 78-79
ruach, 31n4

salvation, 7, 9, 10, 45, 72, 73
Sankofa, 55-56
Sarah, 78
Schüssler Fiorenza, Elisabeth,
  58n19
Scripture. *See also* inerrancy and
    infallibility, doctrines of
  inspiration of, 9-10, 65, 96-98
  translation of, 64, 65-70, 72-74
self-love, redemptive, 21
seminary training, 14-15, 19, 31, 33,
  52, 93
sexuality, Black female, 22-24
shame, 45-49, 51-52, 60, 93-94
Shields, Todd, 38, 39, 40
slavery, in US, 22-23
social justice engagement, 3
Society of Biblical Literature, 13
solidarity, culture of, 48-49
sōma, 79

Southern Baptist Convention, 33–34, 35
Southern Strategy, 32, 37, 38–39
subjective genitive, 72–73
subjectivity, radical, 21
suffering, redemptive, 23
Suicidal Gaul, The, 75, 76f, 77

theology, Christian, 23–24
theopneustos, 96, 97
theōreō, 58
transformation, 28, 86–87
translation of Scripture, 64–70, 72–74
Trump, Donald, 4, 36, 38, 40, 42, 46

"upright" positionality, 45–46, 60

victim blaming, 22–23
victimhood, culture of, 48–49

Walker, Alice, 20–21
Walker-Barnes, Chanequa, 63
"walking in the faith of Jesus" *vs.* "faith in Jesus Christ," 63, 82–87, 92, 94
Weems, Renita, 19

"white as snow," 67–68
White evangelicals, 6, 33–37, 39, 40–42, 93
White supremacist authoritarianism, 6–7, 31–32, 45–46. *See also* biblical interpretation, White supremacist authoritarianism in
White supremacist authority, 7n4
White supremacy, 6, 11, 39. *See also* Southern Strategy
WIC (Special Supplemental Nutritional Program for Women, Infants, and Children), 57n16
Wimbush, Vincent, 91–92
Womanism, 20–21. *See also* biblical interpretation, Womanist; biblical scholarship, Womanist
Womanist air, 96–99
Women and Jesus in Mark (Kinukawa), 58n19
Women in Mark's Gospel (Miller), 58n19

Yang, Seung Ai, 26, 29, 40, 93
Young, Stephen, 34